Stinking Creek

JOHN FETTERMAN has been a newspaperman and freelance writer for seventeen years. He is also a professional photographer. His work has appeared in *Life, The National Observer,* and many other publications. He recently won a Pulitzer Prize for a piece of reporting on Appalachia. A native Kentuckian, Mr. Fetterman lives with his wife and two daughters in Louisville, Kentucky. He says of this volume: "By listening with some compassion and reporting without bias, rather than categorizing, 'experting' or evaluating the hillbilly, the book gives an honest look at the sights, sounds, smells of a hollow in Appalachia. Instead of offering yet another 'solution' for the poor of Appalachia, it spells out in detail just who these people are."

STINKING CREEK was first published in 1967.

STINKING CREEK

JOHN FETTERMAN

A Dutton Paperback

E. P. DUTTON & CO., INC.

NEW YORK   1970

For. L. J. Hortin
who said, "Write the truth."

This paperback edition of

"STINKING CREEK"

First published 1970 by E. P. Dutton & Co., Inc.

Material in Chapter 10 has appeared in the *National Observer*.

Contents

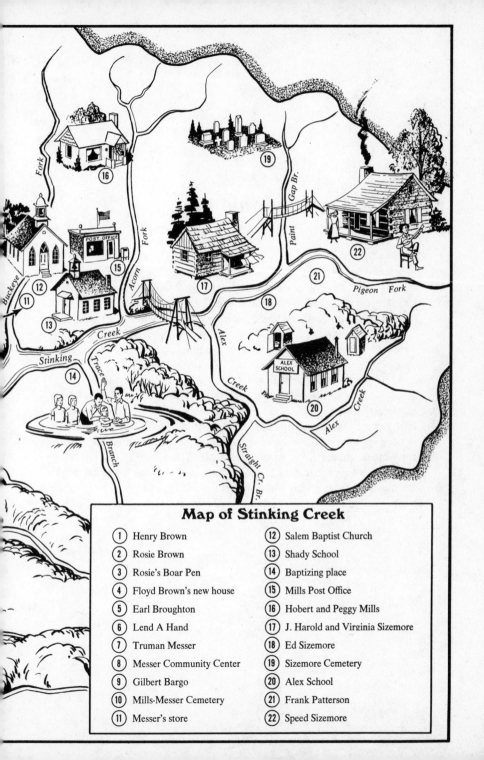

Map of Stinking Creek

1. Henry Brown
2. Rosie Brown
3. Rosie's Boar Pen
4. Floyd Brown's new house
5. Earl Broughton
6. Lend A Hand
7. Truman Messer
8. Messer Community Center
9. Gilbert Bargo
10. Mills-Messer Cemetery
11. Messer's store

12. Salem Baptist Church
13. Shady School
14. Baptizing place
15. Mills Post Office
16. Hobert and Peggy Mills
17. J. Harold and Virginia Sizemore
18. Ed Sizemore
19. Sizemore Cemetery
20. Alex School
21. Frank Patterson
22. Speed Sizemore

Acknowledgments

MUCH OF THE material in this book is from personal interviews, or rather "visits" with hospitable mountain people who welcomed an inquisitive stranger into their hollow, their homes and their church. Other material is from personal observations formed during many trips to the mountains in search of more specific "stories" for newspapers and magazines—observations which became as obsessive and as punishing as the silent, eloquent eyes of the people who live there.

Many people have helped, but I want to mention two in particular: Harry Caudill, a tall, angry mountain lawyer, legislator and author, whose pleas for his native hills, more than any other single factor, have turned eyes toward Appalachia. It was Caudill, sitting in his Spartan office in Whitesburg, Kentucky, in the winter of 1963, the bleak hills visible through the window behind him, who first told me of the hillbilly, an incredible story which I never stopped pursuing. And my wife, who graciously made the transition from golfing widow to writing widow.

J.F.

Foreword

by Harry M. Caudill, Whitesburg, Kentucky

THE PEOPLE WHO settled the southern Appalachians were of a fierce and solitary character, cherishing their freedom and independence as few people ever have. The circumstances which drew them out of Europe and their struggles in the New World made them into radicals and dissenters. They were unprepared to bear the yoke of authority and proclaimed their independence of the Crown more than a year before Jefferson's Declaration of Independence was approved by the Continental Congress. In Mechlenburg County, North Carolina, in May, 1775, the first American "Resolutions of Separation" were adopted by a large assembly of western backwoodsmen. Five years later these frontiersmen met a British army at King's Mountain, South Carolina, and crushed it in what was probably the most resounding defeat ever sustained by a British imperial force.

After the Revolution these people and their kin spread across the Appalachians. They moved into a labyrinth of hills and valleys, streams and forests—and lost themselves within its fastnesses. The labyrinth repelled the rest of the world, and for a century the American Democracy developed largely without their participation, except for the horrible interval of the Civil War which drew them in great numbers into both of the contending armies.

Thus isolated, the mountaineer perpetuated with few changes or improvements the mores, attitudes and practices of the North Carolina and Pennsylvania border of 1775. Few strangers visited him. Few new ideas seeped in to him. His culture congealed and locked him in a perpetual neofrontier.

The world ignored the mountaineer as he ignored it. Perhaps the first mention of the Southern highlander in American literature appears in a

9

tale by Edgar Allan Poe in which he referred to the "fierce and uncouth races of men" dwelling in Western Virginia.

When Horace Kephart came to North Carolina from New England early in this century, he was astounded to find an entire segment of the American people about whom there was no literature. He could find not even so much as a magazine article written within the preceding generation to describe the Southern highlands and their inhabitants. He found no histories or novels that showed an intimate local knowledge of either. He declared, "Had I been going to Teneriffe or Timbuctu, the libraries would have furnished information aplenty; but about this housetop of eastern America they were strangely silent; it was terra incognita."

Kephart remained in the Great Smokies for many years and in 1913 published *Our Southern Highlanders,* almost certainly the best commentary to date on Poe's "fierce and uncouth races of men." His characters lived in the shadow of Clingman's dome, Mount Mitchell, Guyot, Le Conte and the Blacks, but they were of the same breed and stamp as the people farther west in the smaller mountains of Kentucky. His descriptions could have been drawn from life in any one of a thousand east Kentucky communities.

After Kephart's great work, the region's isolation was broken by roads and railways and by countless traumatic intrusions. The federal government bought large areas from which it expelled the people in order to preserve the land as public forests. Lumber companies acquired equally huge tracts and set legions of mountaineers to work cutting down and hauling away the magnificent trees. Forest fires spread across the semicleared ridges and the land eroded with unimaginable speed. Huge corporations bought the rich deposits of coal, iron ore, limestone, oil and gas, and armies of mountaineers were inducted into mines to labor alongside men drawn from many states and from Europe. The southern highlands were swept by a tornado of change.

And in the half century that followed Kephart's work, the mountaineer was betrayed countless times. To begin with, he was betrayed by his ancestors who foolishly sold a gigantic wealth of timber and minerals for only a few pennies to the acre, thus effectively disinheriting whole generations. He was betrayed by the timber barons who exploited the forests with remorseless cupidity, and by the coal corporations which emptied and scarred his hillsides, contaminated his streams with mine acids, polluted his air with sulfurous fumes from burning culm heaps, maimed thousands of workmen and spread multitudes of widows and orphans across the valleys. He was betrayed by his politicians who conspired with the

great, absentee-owned extractive industries to permit them to withdraw
the riches of the mountains without being taxed to provide the schools,
libraries, hospitals and other services for which the mountaineers hungered.
He was betrayed by the mission schools and colleges which came to
educate his children and taught them to leave the region rather than to
stand and fight for its development or, in the case of those few who actually
remained, failed to inspire them to lead their people in the building of a
society worthy of their heritage. And this betrayal is saddest of all, because
in county after county the little cadre of lawyers, doctors and politicians
who can boast of a college education are generally staunch defenders of
the status quo and of those who plunder the region. Rarely is one encountered who advocates the cause of the mountaineer or his land.

And now, half a century after Kephart's time, the mountaineer has been
discovered anew. In the interval, a considerable literature has accumulated
about him and much more is likely to ensue. As the land has deteriorated,
the people have descended with it, and today the most poverty-stricken
counties in America are in our southern highlands—in western Virginia,
West Virginia, eastern Tennessee, eastern Kentucky, and northern Alabama.

If one visits the Indian Reservation at Cherokee, North Carolina, and
gets away from the neon-lit "tourist attractions," he will be dismayed to
find a remnant of the Cherokee nation living in flimsy shacks in the mountain coves. Typically, each shack is surrounded by an accumulation of
trash and junk. The schools are poor, the people underemployed, under-
educated, sullen and hopeless.

And this reservation does not end with the Indians. It spreads westward
and to the south and north for hundreds of miles. This whole vast territory
has been turned into a sprawling reservation with the white people living
amid the same squalor and demoralization as that which afflicts the Cherokee remnant. As the land has yielded its wealth, as the social cripples have
multiplied and as the long betrayal has continued, the region has lost its
social and economic underpinnings. A small measure of prosperity can be
found in the county seats, but the rural populace in the countless hollows
have adopted the welfare rolls as a way of life. Today in dozens of counties,
"welfarism" is the chief industry, providing far more dollars than agriculture, logging or mining.

The debasement of the mountaineer is a tragedy of epic proportions. It
is the story of America's most calamitous failure.

John Fetterman has written a compelling sequel to Kephart's *Our
Southern Highlands*. His work is that of a man fascinated by his subject—

a people, their land, and their melancholy history. He writes as Kephart did, from intimate firsthand knowledge, from long and careful observation and with infinite sympathy and understanding. And, in my opinion, his work is the better of the two, dealing as it does with the mountaineers as they are today in this year of our Lord 1967 on Stinking Creek in Knox County, Kentucky, and on ten thousand other such meandering valleys in an area as big as England.

Kephart has told us what the mountaineers were and John Fetterman has told us what they are. With uneasy conscience we shall look to the future to see what they shall become.

Stinking Creek

1 Prologue—A Dedication

ANYONE WHO LIVES along the banks of an Appalachian stream—such as Stinking Creek—is known as a hillbilly.

Stinking Creek has its source in a lush and lonely marshy spot near the top of a mountain that stands sentinel between the counties of Knox and Clay in Kentucky. At birth, the creek is a silvery ribbon of rippling water timidly venturing forth to keep its rendezvous with the Cumberland River. Within a few yards of its beginning, Stinking Creek begins to trace a tortuous course among the watchful homes of the hillbillies. As it flows it grows in size, fed by countless trickles that drain the highland watershed.

The hillbilly comes from these isolated, beautiful mountains and hollows of Appalachia, and like the land he lives on, he is torn and bleeding, and has lived without hope or champion. The descendant of strong men who wrested the wealth of the mountains from the Indians and then defended it from the British, he sits disconsolately in poverty. His name is on everyone's lips. Kind old ladies in Des Moines, Parent-Teacher groups in New York, drunks in the bars of Los Angeles, professors in our universities—all are worried about the hillbilly. And thus we all have become "experts" in what to do about his plight.

But who is he?

Is he the indolent comic-strip character who sits in filth and mouths earthy witticisms?

Is he an animal-like creature who reproduces at an alarming rate, drinks to excess, and lives without respect for society and its laws?

Is he a stoic, hard-laboring man, jealous of his independence, who heroically spends his strength trying to scratch a living from his barren hills?

Is he an atheist who lives by the creed of the moonshine still and the hog rifle?

Is he a man with a deep faith in an eternal God, a man who lives only for the rewards of the hereafter?

The hillbilly is none—or all—of these things.

The hillbilly is a hillbilly merely because he happens to live in a geographic area where everyone is a hillbilly. He no more follows the stereotype of the hillbilly than does every Texan the stereotype of the swaggering, loud-mouthed Texan. Just as there are New Yorkers who live in penthouses and New Yorkers who exist in slums, there are hillbillies who live in almost every conceivable kind of rural circumstance.

Actually, a hillbilly rarely lives upon a hill. He lives in a hollow. All hollows are basically the same: high mountain walls thrown up on either side by a whimsical nature millions of years ago; at the bottom of the fold in the land runs a stream that drains the watershed. The small hollows that begin high and near the tops of the mountain chains feed their streams into larger streams, which in turn flow along the floors of larger hollows. Along these streams, with the mountains soaring both behind and before him, the hillbilly dwells.

In Appalachia there are thousands of such hollows, each with its own winding stream. All the hollows have two things in common: the streams become larger as they near their rendezvous with the larger streams they serve as tributaries, and the people at the mouths of these larger hollows and streams are more affluent.

As you walk farther and farther up the hollow, both the size of the stream and the standards of living decline steadily. There are bathrooms in Appalachia—and television sets and radios and magazines and newspapers. But not many of these refinements find their way far up to the heads of the hollows.

So in judging the social, political and financial status of a hillbilly, it is not enough to ask, "Are you a hillbilly?"

One also must ask, "How far up the hollow do you come from?"

Or, as the hillbilly himself often asks, "Whose boy are you?"

He knows that whether you reply Jones or Smith or Brown, he can pinpoint your distance up the hollow, and its corresponding degree of isolation from the main road to the county seat. The difference has as great a meaning to him as does the difference between Harlem and Park Avenue to the New Yorker.

The word "hillbilly" is most often applied to the Kentuckian who lives in the hollows of East Kentucky. Surely we have had enough of attempting to analyze the East Kentuckian. Television and radio crews, reporters from New York and a dozen other cities, writers for the slick magazines, news-

Stinking Creek near Lost Fork

men from abroad—all have made a fast trip to East Kentucky for the edification of their viewers and readers.

Along Highway 80, which slashes through the saddened hills from Manchester to Hyden to Hazard to Hindman, the newsmen flock. Their purpose: "I'm here to get some poverty stuff. Mac." And the brakes of their cars squeal day after day at the same "picturesque" spots where shabby little cabins perch and grubby children play.

"Jesus Christ, stop and let me get a coupla shots of that."

"Boy! That's real poverty stuff there."

And on the highway from Jenkins to Whitesburg and from Whitesburg to Harlan, the small motels now serve a cosmopolitan clientele. The taciturn motel manager watches you unload a typewriter and a pair of cameras, sees you are alone, and says disparagingly, "Had a whole N.B.C. crew here last week."

Many newsmen prowl the mountains of East Kentucky to "get some poverty stuff." Poverty is "hot." It is a subject rarely rejected by editors, and poverty stories and pictures are highly salable, as every free-lancer has learned. And easy to obtain. Naïve, curious, and trusting, gaunt mountain men and women pour out tales of suffering, hunger, and privation. Some are true; others only whining recitations offered in the hope that somehow it may increase the monthly welfare check.

Other mountain folk stubbornly insist, "We're making out jest fine." These are the disappearing remnants of a people whose pride and independence are eroding and decaying, just as the hills about them are eroding and decaying, silting and poisoning their streams and destroying their sparse tillable bottom land.

The more one sees of East Kentucky, the more baffling are its people and its desolation. So in February of 1965 the road led again into East Kentucky. This time the visitor had a restive, vague determination to write a book and try to reveal—if only for self-edification—something of what the hillbilly is really like. On the first day, the venture began at a town named Barbourville. The time was shortly before noon on a sunny Saturday morning in mid-February, and the town was filled with people, all obviously in a festive mood.

Around the courthouse square, people in denim, cotton, and khaki milled, laughed, and shouted greetings. Knots of elderly mountain men haggled and lied in the endless ritual of swapping pocket knives. The enthusiastic, discordant sounds of a high-school band came from the courthouse.

It was a great day in the history of Knox County, Kentucky, the day of dedication of the new courthouse. The yellow-brick edifice squatted haughtily in the center of the town square. It had cost half a million dollars, a tidy sum—even if it was largely government money—in a county where children sometimes whimpered with hunger in the cold and dark of February nights.

A county-courthouse dedication, reason dictated, is as good a place as any to begin a book. Wide stairs led to a big, airy circuit-court room on the second floor where the ceremony was under way. It was an impressive sight. A perfumed lady wearing a bright blue dress and matching eye makeup smiled a greeting at the door and distributed printed programs. The judge's bench was lined with local dignitaries, and the stout chairs of the jury box were honored with the broad bottoms of the squires of the county fiscal court, officeholders, and others of local note. There was a scent of flowers, as well as an air of expectation.

The ranking guests of honor—the Honorable Tim Lee Carter, Congressman from the Fifth District of Kentucky, and the Honorable John Sherman Cooper, United States Senator from Kentucky—were not present as promised on the printed program.

The people sitting in the courtroom and smiling under the yellow rays of the winter sun that poured through the tall windows were quite unlike those gathered outside. Inside, a well-fed, content air and a liberal scattering of neckties were in evidence. Outside were some shabbiness and considerably more unshaven faces. But this apparent lack of complete representation in the courtroom did not detract from the exuberance of the occasion.

There were glowing tributes to those who had made the magnificent building possible, a structure hailed by one orator as "a new beginning to meet the new times facing us in Kentucky." And the oblong brick building was called "the symbol of a pact between the people and their government."

Since the two dignitaries who were to head the array of political conquerors were not at hand, a substitute was necessary for the principal address. This is never a problem of great concern in Kentucky, where every courthouse is alive with orators, all of whom know the few basic orations by heart. In this instance, the Honorable B. Robert Stivers, Judge of the Twenty-seventh Judicial District of Kentucky, was hurled into the breach, and performed creditably. A compact, virile man, the judge proved to be of journeyman stature in the craft of Kentucky courthouse speaking. From the recognition of the local leadership present to the acknowledgment of his great thanksgiving for the privilege of serving them under civil government, His Honor's full, moist tones fell upon an approving audience.

Outside, citizens obviously of lesser social and political stature also appeared pleased. In the manner of mountain men, they already were anointing the gleaming white steps and foundations of the new building with the brown blessing of tobacco juice. Spitting, haggling, laughing, just as they had blessed the ninety-one-year-old edifice of government that preceded it in the deliberate history of Knox County, Kentucky.

In the courtroom, the time came for the judge to inject a light note into his speech. "Every circuit judge in Kentucky should have Knox County for one month—and Stinking Creek for three months," he said. There was a titter of laughter, an elbowing of neighbors, and a few sharp cackles of merriment.

Stinking Creek? Perhaps a place to begin. And Stinking Creek was where the quest both began and ended.

This, then, is the story of a few hillbillies who lived at a particular time in history along a creek called Stinking in a particular hollow almost lost among the thousands of hollows of Appalachia. This is a part of what might have been seen and heard and learned by anyone willing to walk many times up Stinking Creek and see the people who lived there. Or, more important, listen with compassion to the people who lived there.

2 How They Got There

THERE ARE TWO peoples whose journeys through the centuries have followed similar tortuous paths.

One group is called Jews, and their history is one of bondage, struggle against oppression, wandering in the wilderness, suffering and discrimination. The Jews at length encountered a man named Hitler who espoused a "final solution" to the Jewish problem. It was neither final nor a solution.

Another group is called hillbillies, and their history is one of bondage, struggle against oppression, wandering in the wilderness, suffering and discrimination. They came at length to the hollows of Appalachia, and now have encountered a solution. The solution is called "The War on Poverty."

The Jews produced a teacher; the hillbillies are among the few today who still believe literally what He taught.

Of the Jews it is said, "They endured privation and suffering."

An elderly hillbilly complained, "Brother, if there is a shitty end of a stick to hand somebody, they seem bound and determined to hand it to us."

Most schoolboys learn in school—or by watching television—that Daniel Boone came first to Kentucky. Actually, Ol' Daniel, who today would probably be branded as a child deserter, thus enabling his wife to qualify for aid to dependent children, was a late arrival upon the scene. Other men, driven by more intense desires and with greater longing for the freedom of isolation, first saw Stinking Creek and the other teeming streams of the Kentucky hills. They were impressed by what they found for two reasons. It was wild, lush country rich in game, fish, and timber. And, regardless of what they found, they could only improve themselves. Their heritage was better forgotten.

A mountaineer when asked how his ancestors came to this place answered, "They walked."

True, they walked. But as they walked they fought—the Choctaw, the

21

Shawnee, the wild animals, and each other. In a country where only the most savage could survive, the mountaineer survived. His historic enemies are dead and gone. The mountaineer was a savage man because his heritage was savagery. Of English, Scottish, and Irish descents, he came, not as a clean-cut, wholesome, educated explorer, but as a man scarred by years of abuse.

In England the debtor prisons were brimming. Orphans roamed the filthy streets. There were plantations in the Carolinas and Virginia in need of workers. Just as Americans enslaved the black men, they enslaved the derelicts from the "old countries." Bonded, beaten, despised, these forebears of the hillbilly knew nothing of the arts of the craftsmen, the cunning of the merchants, the skills of the tradesmen. Their inheritance was a feeble spark of hope that they might escape their ordeal.

For years there have been those who insist that the selling of mountain crafts is a way to bring financial stability to the mountains. Mountain crafts are hideously unsightly. The doodads made of cedar saplings and peddled as "mountain crafts" are tasteless and dull. Because this is not the hillbillies' inheritance. No silversmiths crossed the mountains. No artisans.

But fighters did cross. Strong men. Men burning with a passion to escape the authority created to punish and destroy them in Britain, and later another authority half a world away in a new country. By the time the authority in the New World was being formalized on a piece of paper stipulating that "all men are created equal," the hillbillies were already pushing into the western wilderness where the mountains touched the sky. Fleeing the plantations, they were itching to move westward when a gap was discovered in the Cumberland Mountains in 1750. So the mountain settlers who already were at the edge of nowhere in the mountains of Virginia fled even farther west. At a place called Flat Lick, Kentucky, there is a shallow place in the Cumberland River, and many crossed there. Flat Lick is less than an hour's walk from Stinking Creek.

Here the Long Hunters crossed, so named because of the long periods of time they spent hunting in the mountains. On one expedition, the Long Hunters killed a bear, ate what they could, and threw the carcass into the creek. In time, there arose a stench. From then on, the creek was called Stinking Creek, and was so marked on the first crude maps.

The Long Hunters were followed closely by the settlers, and at times the settlers were, in fact, Long Hunters returning to settle and claim lands that had struck their fancy.

There were teachers to heed. The Indian taught new applications of wilderness cunning, how to plant, how to build a cabin. The beasts taught caution and the importance of swift killing.

By 1800 there were hundreds of such settlers across the Kentucky mountains. Each family was an entity to itself; it provided its own vegetables and meat, treated its own wounds and ills, killed its own enemies, made its own corn whiskey.

A distant shot, heard faintly across the misty mountains, was enough to cause a frontiersman to pack up his belongings and move on to less crowded quarters. With the father leading the way, the family moved, carrying its meager tools and possessions, until at length the head of the group cast down his load, and announced, "We'll build here." His word was law. He made the rules and punished the violators.

Throughout the eighteenth century, these hardy folk arrived, fought the Indians—or married them—and sought their destiny in the lush new land. The timber was burned to create patches for corn and tobacco; fish were pulled from the streams, and game was hunted with a tenacity beyond the Indian's wildest dreams. But there was plenty.

The mountaineer also was independent in another field—religion. Whether he could read or had to have someone read the Bible to him, he formulated his own theology. He was distrustful of the established churches (they were affiliated with the Crown)—but at times waves of evangelistic fervor swept the mountains. The fervor was of a fundamental brand of religion the mountaineer could understand and trust. It was a fatalistic creed. If an ax accidentally severed a foot, "It was the Lord's will." When a beast mangled or killed a child, "It was the Lord's will."

When the Revolutionary War came, the mountaineer, with family-told tales of abuse at the hands of the Crown gnawing at his mind, volunteered eagerly. Dismissed as "riffraff" by the regulars, he fought well. The mountaineer's woodsmanship and eagerness for the kill soon dispelled any notions that his tales of frontier adventures were imaginary. His fame was made at the Battle of Kings Mounain, when mountain sharpshooters slaughtered their disciplined adversaries.

From this war, a grateful Congress—long on unexplored land and short on cash—evolved a system of paying its veterans with tracts of land "in the West." In Knox County, the records show, veterans of the war who came to settle bore such names as Isaac Messer, John Messer, Job Broughton, William Patterson, Rowland Brown, William Brown, and William Collitt. These family names are borne by people who live on Stinking Creek today. Many of them live much as their ancestors lived: in families that are near in terms of distance, but far apart in terms of community living. They are not, as portrayed for decades in Sunday supplements and occasional feature articles, sagacious men who whittle endless piles of cedar shavings and speak deep truths in the form of legendary anecdotes. Neither are they a sullen collection of suspicious, treacherous men, as they are sometimes described. They are not outwardly emotional, except in occasional religious outbursts, and their stoicism is sometimes misinterpreted as stupidity. They are not a learned group.

But the contemporary hillbilly does have traits that seem to be disappearing in the society from which the mountains sheltered him. And an increasing knowledge of these traits prompts the question:

"Do they contain anything the world needs today?"

3 Land of Coal and Old Men

THE RECENT HISTORY of the land the hillbilly lives upon is paradox piled upon paradox. The greatest and most central paradox is East Kentucky itself. Here lies a region of poverty, ignorance, and rebellion sheltered by mountains bursting with untold riches in coal, gas, oil, and other resources. East Kentucky is a land where men sit on the sagging porches of their shabby homes, feel the gnawing of hunger in their bellies, and watch the black wealth of coal pour from the mountains around them.

In East Kentucky, county governments struggle along on anemic fiscal budgets that are inadequate to maintain their shoddy roads and shameful schools—while wealth pours past their eyes in the form of coal en route to the markets of the nation.

With almost masochistic pleasure, East Kentucky has ruined its mountains with rapacious mining practices, eroded its slopes, polluted its streams, leveled its timber, and turned a land of plenty into a bleak region for welfare recipients. There are still more than thirty-three billion tons of coal to be mined in East Kentucky. By the time it is removed, the area will be totally unfit for human habitation.

This appears to alarm no one. Kentucky has long prided itself on its childish "politics," and Kentucky's lack of political leadership is legendary. In an age when other men look to the era of space and a world of nuclear marvels, Kentuckians sit enthralled by their leaders who harp on the ancient litany of love of "God, motherhood, and good roads." But perhaps it is well that they do. If statistics could be gathered on these three worthy endeavors, Kentucky would probably find itself at the bottom of the list, just as it usually does when most other national ratings are announced.

Diverse topics lie temptingly open to those who dwell upon the plight of the mountains.

There is geology—including those ancient ferns and plants that became the peat that became the seams of coal.

There is politics—the decades of shouting and breast-beating that led nowhere.

There is the fiscal problem—a medicine show of pathetic proportions that has cringed at even token taxation of the wealth removed from the state.

But let us turn to the land itself and the people who exist upon it. This requires few statistics, those long columns of hocus-pocus that delight the researcher.

Now that the mountaineer has made the perilous journey from the debtor prisons of England to the lushness of Appalachia, most of what has happened to him since can be observed by merely walking into his region and looking . . . and smelling . . . and listening.

The hillbilly is a mountaineer without mountains, and the gullies of erosion in his spirit and soul are as evident as are the gaping wounds in the hills around him. The visible parallel of simultaneous destruction of hill and human being is shattering.

The mining of coal is a profitable business. Coal taxes are practically non-existent at the state level except through a loose income-tax requirement. On the federal level, depletion allowance and capital-gains provisions further boost the profit potential. But, as any Kentuckian will tell you, all this goes "outside." "Outside" is an array of national corporations, landholding companies, and investors.

Long ago the settlers in Appalachia sold their rights to the minerals. This was done through the "long deeds," wordy documents that gave up all rights at the going rate—usually fifty cents an acre. The long deeds further decreed that whoever held title could take timber, pollute or divert streams, destroy buildings, level mountains, choke valleys—in fact take any step necessary to get at the mineral wealth they had acquired. The courthouses of eastern Kentucky are full of these ancient deeds, many signed with an *X,* and to read them would make Jesse James blush.

But the mere taking of the minerals was not a disaster, the manner in which they are being taken is the blow from which East Kentucky may never recover.

In the early days of coal mining, the region boomed. Those were the days of the deep mine, when men went below the earth to dig and shovel and haul away the black gold. The valleys rocked to the shouts and laughter of the miners. Thousands upon thousands of men earned good wages even while the rest of the state was worried about unemployment. The mountaineer forsook his rifle and plow, took up the pick and shovel, and prospered.

But mining techniques changed. The bulldozer was invented, and the coal auger. It has become a simple matter to reach and remove a seam of coal with a dozen men—instead of hundreds. Automation has made the miner jobless. And as the mines rejected him, so did his union, for which he had picketed, fought, and even died. So the mountaineer became another paradox: an unemployed and unemployable industrial worker in a wilderness setting.

To reach the coal seams now, a bulldozer strips the earth from the seam, following the black ore around the contour of a mountain. This leaves a gash, similar to a cut made for a road. Power shovels scoop up the coal that lies exposed. Augers—huge rotating bits up to seven feet in diameter—bore into the mountain to bring out the remainder of the seam, much as wood curls up from a boring wood auger.

The resulting tons of waste—earth, slate, and slag—are hurled over the mountainside in an orgy of monstrous ruin.

Sulfur, associated with coal-bearing formations, enters the streams, and a solution of sulfuric acid results. The silt washes down the mountainsides to fill the stream beds, and during heavy rains the valleys act as huge funnels, hurling the unchecked waters along to inundate town after town.

Flooding, from streams whose beds are choked with silt, is a way of life in East Kentucky—something to be lived with and expected. In Hazard, one of the more prosperous county seats, some merchants are three loans deep into the seasonal assistance they get from the Small Business Administration to help pay for sweeping out the flood debris and returning to business.

The slag, which is tossed over the mountainside from strip mines and coal-washing installations, sometimes ignites and burns for months, killing vegetation and filling the air with a sulfurous stench. To come upon the horror of one of these simmering, spewing mountains is like plunging into Dante's Inferno. When the rains come in the spring and fall, the huge "gob" piles from the mines give way and ooze into the valleys below to destroy homes, fields, and creeks.

Wildlife has disappeared. The poisonous, silt-laden streams run bright red with iron precipitate or frothy white with sulfur. They are highly acid—even to the point of deteriorating concrete—and fish have forsaken them. Hundreds of streams bear biological poisons that kill the wildlife and plants they touch.

"There ain't even a crawdad around here," an old-timer observed.

Kentucky conservationists long have been shocked at the grotesque spectacle of a verdant region literally devouring itself. But until recently, their determined cries of protest have been ignored in the halls of government of a plundered state.

On the lower levels of state government, where a few men are concerned with conservation of timber, fish, and wildlife, there are heroic efforts at land reclamation. They point out that turbidity in the water keeps the game fish from their daily rounds of sight feeding, and obscures the rocky bottoms where they lay eggs. So the fish are no more. Others bewail the pollution in the streams, where raw sewage spews its ghastly load of coliform bacteria, the warning signal of virus and disease and epidemic. Others look at the naked hills and suggests reforestation.

But for the most part their efforts are futile. They are not the men who control the destiny of the hills.

Meanwhile, the spokesmen for the coal industry prate of their concern for the natural wonders they desecrate, and piously lead "the press" on pilgrimages to tiny green "demonstration reclamation projects" where blades of foliage are coaxed into life amid the ruins. Sometimes the press is impressed, and the industry is clothed in a mantle of threadbare respectability—like the trite, worn cloak of understanding in which writers drape the "prostitute with a heart of gold."

And all the while, the tortured mountains groan and settle into the cavities left by the auger. The scream of the auger's cutting edge as it rapes the mountains and the throaty voice of the bulldozer as it nudges its load over the mountainside are the sounds the mountaineer hears daily.

There are eight million mountaineers left in Appalachia. Many are leaving. But some are staying—in determination or in despair.

Knox County is not the worst of the mountain counties. Nor is it the best. It is merely the county where one day they dedicated a courthouse and where one day a decision was made to visit a place called Stinking Creek.

The Kentucky Department of Commerce and the Knox County Chamber of Commerce have caused to be published a bold little booklet extolling "Industrial Resources, Barbourville, Kentucky." It reveals that the 1960 census credited Knox County with 25,258 living souls, of whom 3,211 live in Barbourville, the county seat. It further advises that 1,187 men and 1,511 women are available as a labor supply.

Barbourville, the booklet says, is 493 miles from Chicago, 388 miles from

Detroit, and 829 miles from New York. The study makes the statement, "The inhabitants of Knox County are primarily engaged in agriculture." We shall see.

The booklet also makes other information available to interested industrial planners:

• The average weekly earnings during 1961 were $51.89 for all industries and $47.20 for manufacturing. During the same period the state average was $83.44 for all industries and $96.07 for manufacturing.

• In 1960, per capita income for Knox County was $501; per capita income for Kentuck was $1,573, far below the national average of $2,223. Knox County ranked 119th among Kentucky's 120 counties and Kentucky ranked 46th among the 50 states.

• The largest employer in Barbourville is a firm which manufacturers brassieres and employs around 150 people.

• Knox County operates on an annual budget of something over $125,000.

• The net assessed value of property in Knox County was given as $14,331,725.

But Knox County is not primarily in the agricultural business, nor is it in the timber business or the coal business, or the brassiere business: Knox County, like all counties of Appalachia, is in the welfare business. And business is great.

Of the 6,500 dwelling units, only 10 percent have plumbing, and about 6 percent of the 20,625 acres of crop land is in good condition. More than 64 percent of the population receives some kind of welfare assistance—not counting medical aid. About half of the lunches in the school lunch programs are served free, because children cannot pay the price of ten cents.

The pursuit of welfare figures is a maddening quest. Even veteran soldiers in the War on Poverty must run their computers at full throttle to keep abreast of the barrage of welfare checks aimed at conquering poverty. But during the development of this book, the following figures were suggested by the Kentucky Department of Economic Security, which administers many welfare programs:

In one month, 3,057 recipients in Knox County were handed $117,585. In a month, nearly 900 aged persons received more than $52,000; 64 of the needy blind received nearly $5,000; 194 disabled persons collected more than $14,000; more than $38,182 was handed out as aid to dependent children; and unemployed fathers, with a total of more than 1,200 children, were paid around $44,000. In Knox County, 119 claimants for unemployment insurance collected on a state average of $33.59. In a month, social-security recipients were paid more than $141,000.

In addition, Knox County enjoyed the benefits of projects under the Area Redevelopment Administration and the Accelerated Public Works program (such as the new courthouse). Furthermore, a new jungle of federal bene-fits has begun to germinate under the careful tending of the Office of Economic Opportunity.

In Knox County the collecting of welfare benefits has far outstripped the manufacture of brassieres as the backbone of the economy.

Perhaps the most basic and interesting of all the phenomena of the wel-fare county is the surplus-commodity program. Its administration is simple. A family gets itself approved, is issued a card, and from then on it collects its fair share of the nation's food bounty once a month.

In Knox County, as this is written, 8,461 people enjoy these benefits. The surplus commodities are distributed in a dingy little building on the eastern outskirts of the city to ragtag descendants of men who would fight to the death rather than "be beholden to any man."

In a year, a quarter of a million Kentuckians were given 56,000,000 pounds of surplus foodstuffs that had an estimated wholesale value of around $13,000,000. The recipient families draw a monthly average of around 100 pounds of powdered milk, rice, meal, flour, lard, dried eggs, butter, canned beef and pork, cheese, beans, peanut butter, and occasional cans of fruit.

The commodity food programs are administered on the local level and are regarded with horror by students of political science for the simple reason that the control of food can lead to the control of votes. Charges and denials, innuendoes and inefficiency, are handmaidens of the program.

As for the commodities themselves, most are of high quality. Unattractiv-ely packaged by the United States Department of Agriculture in brown boxes or stenciled tin cans, the contents are first rate. The beef and pork, cooked in big iron skillets on wood-burning stoves, is delicious. And so is the cheese, which the occasional visitor "bums" for a lunch up a hollow. The peanut butter is also very good. Many mountaineers dislike the rice and do not know how to prepare it. But they all know what to do with the lard, since frying in deep grease is standard procedure.

But children grow tired of the "commodity food," and rebel. Some moun-taineers use the food to trade. Some feed it to the hogs. Others wisely use the commodities as a way to vary their diet of biscuits, coffee, garden beans, corn, and boiled or fried pork.

Stinking Creek is only a part of Knox County. It is neither the best nor the worst part. It is typical of nothing, because every hollow of the thousands in eastern Kentucky bears its own particular characteristics dictated by the nature and size of the creek that drains it, the families that settled it, and the particular array of welfare programs that sustain it.

Stinking Creek is not difficult to find. From Barbourville, U.S. Highway 25-E is a busy, broad, black-topped ribbon that runs eastward toward Pineville and the tourist attractions to the east and south. Seven miles from Barbourville, just after the highway passes the Turkey Creek Mission, a paved road turns to the left. This road follows the creek named Stinking for about twenty miles, changing from blacktop to gravel to mud or dust as it climbs toward the source of the creek high in the narrow fold of a mountain. There are no signposts to identify the many tributaries that enter Stinking Creek and along which other and more remote families live, but their names are vital if one plans to travel the area or discuss it. There is Roaring Fork, a quiet little trickle, which enters beside an ancient rock schoolhouse. To the left, as you travel upstream, there are the major tributaries, Road Fork and then Middle Fork, the valley that leads to Browns Hollow. All along the mainstream of Stinking Creek, the lesser creeks enter quietly and consistently, marking the sites where live the inhabitants of Stinking Creek: Kenningham Branch, where two women live and struggle to serve the people around them; Laurel Creek, where one of the tiny schools sits; Buckeye Fork, where Messer's store and the Salem Baptist Church make the junction a focal point in Stinking Creek life; Acorn Fork, which gurgles into Stinking Creek beside the Mills post office; and farther up into the misty hollow, Pigeon Fork and Paint Gap Branch, where the Sizemores live.

Some of these tiny tributaries come shyly and drably to their rendezvous with Stinking Creek. Others, such as Lost Fork, enter daintily, through spectacularly beautiful wooded hollows. And all the creeks must be known, just as street names must be known, because they mark the beginning and the ending of all journeys. And all have an "upper" side and a "lower" side. So the address you seek is never told in numbers, but merely, "They live on the upper side of Buckeye."

Stinking Creek itself suddenly changes character at a point where it is joined by Alex Creek. Above Alex, Stinking Creek runs clear and blue. Below Alex Creek, the stream is stained with an orange-red deposit and its waters are acid. Below Alex, the round sandstone rocks are perpetually stained and the fish are gone.

Although the coal beneath the slopes that soar away on both sides of

Stinking Creek has not yet been mined, Stinking Creek feels the effects of
the mines. Across the mountain from the source of Alex Creek, water has
been backed into an abandoned mine. At length it burst free on the Stinking
Creek side of its mountain prison, where laden with garish red precipitate
and sulphuric aric, it spews its poison into Alex Creek, which in turn delivers
the loathsome burden into Stinking Creek. Possibly two thirds of the citizens
of Stinking Creek live below Alex Creek, and consequently must live with
a stream that runs pure only in the memories of the older inhabitants.

Stinking Creek is not a community. It is an area of steep slopes and
narrow bottoms sprinkled with homes that range from neat painted clapboard houses—some of them even boasting an inside bathroom—to totter-
ing, sagging little shacks. Each home is a little society unto itself, and many
families find they have little in common with their neighbors. They differ
in their religion, morals, ethics, and their attitudes toward the welfare program. Family bloodlines are complicated; and although there is a deep
feeling of attachment to one's "kin," there is little sense of community
unity.

The head-hanging shyness and suspiciousness often credited to the mountaineer are merely his generations-old habit of keeping his nose out of other
people's business. Outward signs of love—even between husband and wife—
are rare. When affection is shown, it almost always is for the "baby" of the
family or for the oldest member.

Mountain homes, those of the very poor, follow a pattern. A room in
front, one or two double beds, and a sagging couch in front of a television
set being paid for from welfare checks; another room directly behind, full of
beds, dark and musty and always with the feeling of dampness; a small room
or a lean-to used as a kitchen with a wood- or coal-burning stove, a rickety
table, wooden shelves for storing things, and a collection of often-repaired
chairs. There are door facings at all the doors, but rarely are there doors.
Some doorways modestly boast faded strips of cotton material that can be
pulled together for a semblance of privacy.

There is a smell of poverty that is characteristic of many houses along
Stinking Creek: a flat, weary, penetrating aroma of seasoned and rotting
wood, unwashed clothing and bodies. But the smell of poverty is strangely
similar to the smell of prosperous mountain farm homes. Some find it over-
whelmingly insufferable. Others find in the flat, strong smell of human bodies
a sense of permanence, of enduring things. After several days in the hollows,
an elevator filled with ladies in town for a convention is unbearable. The
entrapped reek of oils and perfumes and powders can be more nauseating
than anything encountered in Stinking Creek—or in any hollow.

An outhouse has a stench of its own, of course. But these are neither an invention of, nor peculiar to, the mountains. Outhouses by the thousands are found in other rural areas across our nation—and even in our cities—and they are often regarded as "quaint." It is customary, however, to gasp in disgust at a two-holer in Appalachia as though it were a temple erected to some god of moral degeneration.

The mountaineer is what he is simply because he was born what he is. Each hollow has its moonshine peddlers and loose women and lazy men and complaining women. And each hollow has its courageous men and determined women who battle hopeless odds to bring their broods to a better life. But the best way to know something of Stinking Creek—and thereby something of Appalachia—is to meet and talk with and learn to know some of the people who live there. Not to study them with the idea of categorizing them into meaningless groups, but to sit and listen.

And sooner or later, the mountaineer will ask, "How do you like it here?" Or at a funeral, someone will inquire, "I don't guess you ever seen a preachin' like this?"

The mountaineer would like to have just one person—one day—come into his hollow and show some sign of approval of the way he has lived over the decades, and the way he wants to live forever. And not try to change him without first knowing him. So the purpose here is not to advocate some miraculous cure of the ills of Appalachia. It is merely to meet and know a few of the people who live and work and loaf and hunger and pray along the banks of a little stream called Stinking Creek.

Those who would attempt to separate the citizens of Stinking Creek into two groups could do no better than repeat the words of Golden Slusher:
"What don't work is drawin'."

The majority are "drawin'." They draw welfare checks or commodities or both, and these are the basis of their economic security. The balance are working—for the time being.

Golden Slusher was working. It was a blowing, snowy day, and the warmth from his small coal fireplace was welcome. Slusher is a muscular, quiet man in his forties, and not a talker. But he is hospitable and willing to share his fireplace on a wintry day. The Slushers had no children. Mrs. Slusher, a small, wiry, dark-haired woman, sat silently back near the edge of the circular yellow glow from the fireplace. Nearer the fire sat Mrs. Slusher's mother, Mrs. Betty Smallwood, who is eighty-six and who sits and rocks and silently recollects, and complains of her heart.

Golden Slusher knows better than to try to farm as his ancestors did.

The soil on the ridges above Pigeon Creek is thin and sandy and heavy with gravel. It contains little clay, and cannot retain moisture. The plant-food content is low. There is no level land along the banks of Pigeon Creek.

Golden Slusher is a logger. He arises before dawn, goes to the woods over in Bell County, hitches up the mules he keeps there, and all day strains his still-powerful muscles to drag out the logs that keep him alive—and off the welfare rolls.

"I ain't drawin'. I'm loggin'," he repeats.

But not many men have his stamina.

It is always easiest to talk with the old people, of whom there are many. They know the creek well, and have a serenity from long years of living with the hills, and an instinctive politeness. Most of the old men once worked in the deep mines. The mines killed many of them and maimed many more. To those who worked and lived, the mines left memories that will not die until the last old man dies.

There are many such old men on Stinking Creek. Ed Sizemore and Frank Patterson are two of them.

Ed Sizemore . . . . had his own private coal mine. It was only a small outcropping of coal on the hillside behind his house. But Ed could take a wheelbarrow back there, pick around in the hole he had dug, and return with his own private coal supply. But he doesn't do that much anymore because his back hurts. "If I bend my back it gives me such miseries I can't stand it," he said. He went to work in the mines when he was fourteen, and stayed there until about a year ago.

His present age is a matter of dispute between him and the federal government. Ed is trying to get social security.

Stinking Creek runs directly behind Ed Sizemore's house. A huge boulder sits on the bank to deflect the torrent when the creek is swollen from the spring rains. So far, the boulder has saved his house from each succeeding flood. "It turns the tide right back into the creek," Ed said.

He massaged the small of his back through his loosely fitting overalls, and tried to tell of his difficulties with federal authority. "I don't get a dime from the government," he said. Hurt filled his pale blue eyes. He shuffled his blocky figure beneath the folds of the overalls. "Oh, I got a little compensation when I got hurt. I'm going in front of the doctors agin 'fore long. One's a social-security doctor, too. I got plenty in that social security. Buddy, I worked years and years before social security ever thought of coming in. I was working when the man brought that card up to me for me to sign.

Ed Sizemore

"I said, 'What is it?' It was all green to me.

"I put up most of my life in a mine. I made my living in a hill and raised fourteen kids. Under the union I made good—twenty-five or thirty a day. Under a scab mine you had to really work to get ten a shift.

"Hit'll be a year the sixteenth of this month since I was hurt. I'm old enough to retire, as far as that goes. They sent and got fifty-four as my age. I'm 'way older than that. My mother ought to know my age. Well, I was sixty-two years old two years ago, but they wouldn't have it that way. I just let it go for then. I seen I couldn't do no better.

"The govermint ought to see to a man when he's down and out. But they are hardest on the man who put it in, in the world. He can put it in, but he can't get it out. And nobody in this whole county helped me."

Ed Sizemore remembers the mines well, but not with fondness. Like most old miners, he had a horror that his sons would follow him into the mines. One son did. "Me and one of my boys worked a seam together oncet. I tried and tried to get him not to go back in. He finally quit and went to Detroit. He runs a 'dozer up there."

Ed Sizemore was injured while "robbing" a mine, a practice that has left many a body entombed forever beneath the mountains. As the old deep miners worked farther and farther into a seam, they left pillars of coal to support the treacherous roof of the mine. After the coal was all taken out, the miners would begin to "rob" the mine—take out the supporting pillars. Starting with the pillar farthest back in the mine, they would salvage all that was left, working their way back to the mine mouth and ready to flee for the opening at the first sign of a fault in the roof.

Mining, Ed said, was dangerous enough without having to rob the seams. "The electric cable, for one thing, could kill you deader than thunder, and it did kill some. I done most my mining in Leslie County. You'd lay on your side or get on your knees, anyway you can get to get at the coal. We was robbing. Getting the last of it."

Ed Sizemore cocked his head to look across the creek, and was silent for a long time. Perhaps he was reliving the day when the mine roof came crashing down and put the miseries in his back. But when he turned back, he did not mention robbing a mine again.

His first wife died twenty-three years ago, and that was when he bought his forty acres on Stinking Creek. He quickly remarried. "I couldn't rest easy working in the mines with the kids home by theirself. So I married her. She hope me raise them.

"This is a good spot to live. In forty-seven I had this whole bottom in sweet taters big as your two fists from a goose egg up. They just rot in the

ground, but I had enough left for the winter. I had two big mares, and I had
some old time getting them up that hill out of the tide when the rains come."

The smell of beans cooking had been coming from the house. Now Ed's
wife, a pleasant woman with a broad smile, came to the kitchen door, made
an almost imperceptible signal, and Ed Sizemore eased toward the house.

"Come back any time you take a notion," he said.

Frank Patterson . . . . Frank was sitting on a log in the sunshine up by the
road near his house. The spot is the last place you can turn a car without
climbing all the way to the head of the hollow, and the road was muddy
from a recent rain. Frank's unblinking eyes were fixed on the camera. He
shoved his hat back a bit on his head and said evenly, "Put under that picture, 'Frank Patterson who's lived eighty-two years!' "

In eighty-two years, he has done about everything a man can do on Stinking Creek. He let his eyes sweep across the hills. "I used to farm all those
hills 'till I got wore out . . . and the hills got wore out . . . no timber . . .
no nothin'."

The Pattersons are a big family—or a big "generation," as mountain
people put it. They came to the hollow early, crossing the shallow place in
the Cumberland River, then turning northeastward into the Stinking Creek
watershed. The first Patterson was "old man" John Patterson, Frank's
grandfather.

"There wasn't no record kept of nobody," Frank said. "But John Patterson was the first in. He fought in the old Revolution War and didn't die 'til
after I was married. John was old enough to be using a walking cane, and I
was about twenty when he died. He was a big tall fellow. Weighed about
one seventy-five. He farmed and hunted. John had eight children. My notion
is he came from Tennessee. John married a Golden, Polly Ann Golden. They
used to live up the hill there."

The old man, John Patterson, who had come to live upon his land given
him for his service against the British, did leave a large "generation." There
are many Pattersons in the hollow.

Frank is the oldest Patterson now. And the family records are in his head.

"My daddy was James, or Jim. Jim lived to eighty-four, and my mother
was a Taylor. There were nine of us children." Frank and a sister are the
only survivors of that family.

As was the custom, the family land was divided among the children, then
among the children's children, until the vast mountain holdings dwindled to
tiny plots.

"My mother aired [was heir to] three hundred acres of land, and we divided it up. John had one hundred acres at Messer and sold it out. I own this little bit of property here where I'm livin'."

Frank waved a bony hand toward the bottom below his house, a wide space beside the creek where a square, concrete block one-room school now sits. The name of the school is Erose.

"The county paid me $150 for that bottom. I tried to get out of selling it, but they forced me to. That was going on thirty year ago."

Mrs. Patterson is a small woman, gray and prim, friendly and frank. Her tiny body appears to be buried in layers of cotton petticoats, skirts, and an apron. Her dark eyes are alert and inquisitive. The best single word to describe her, perhaps, is "sweet." If a woman were needed to personify the perfect mountain grandmother, Mrs. Patterson would make an excellent candidate. The Pattersons were sitting on the porch of their sturdy, ancient house. The yard is surrounded by its "palings," a fence of slender slats that encircles and protects the yard.

They sat on the porch, spat out through the porch railings, and talked. Frank said he served his time in the mines.

"I used to work in the mines. Lord, that was dangerous. My God, they got killed every day. Sometimes five and six a day. But people wasn't gettin' no other work. A man'd get killed; another'd take his place."

Mrs. Patterson placed a tiny blue-veined hand on his shoulder. "They didn't make enough to bury them," she said.

Frank sighed. "I worked many a day for seventy-five cents. Oncet I got twenty cents a day to dig that coal. I got bruised up a little, but not no damage much."

His mining days were put in before there were safety regulations or modern machinery, when strong men crawled beneath the mountains and tore the coal out as best they could.

"Those lamps on our caps burned lard oil. They had a little ol' wick, and the smoke stayed in your face all the time. We didn't have no fans to clear the air out. Oncet we dug a channel straight up for fifty feet to the top of the ground. Then we put a furnace under the hole to burn coal in. It would make a draft and draw air in through the drift mouth. If the air got heavy, you'd have to go to where the air was. Times, the air got so dead you couldn't get your breath. Oncet the air was gone and the lamps was jest sparkin' 'stead of burning. I said, 'Let's get out,' and I run to the trapdoor. I was so weak I couldn't open it. I lay down with my face against that door tryin' to get me some air. I got to feelin' better with that air, but I heered my buddy strugglin' back in the coal vein. He was just about gone when I got to him, but I got him out of there."

Mr. and Mrs. Frank Patterson

The mines were no place for Frank Patterson, the grandson of the fighter and hunter who killed deer for his brood of children, farmed and lived under the open sky. As soon as he could, Frank walked away from the darkness and death of the coal mines.

He became a carpenter.

"I'd sit and study the carpenters that people was able to hire 'til I caught on to it myself. We raised nine children with me carpenterin'. I built most every house on the upper end of this creek. I built all the time for other people. I was about all the carpenter there was. I used just old rough lumber, and they'd pay $25 or $30 something along there, to get a house built. It'd take me about a month to build one."

Mrs. Patterson had heard it all many times. But she sat with her thin arms folded in front of her and her dark eyes fixed on her husband. "He built this house," she said with a hint of pride in her soft voice.

"That's right," Frank said. This house been here forty-five years. It was an old log house, just one room. Then I built three more rooms on."

Mrs. Patterson spoke softly and slowly, sometimes pausing to knit her pale brow in concentration, as though she wanted to make sure there would be no inaccuracies: "Lord, I'm seventy-five, and I was Mary Jane Mills. My generation of Mills' lived in Clay County."

Frank interrupted. "I think we got eighty grandchildren."

Mrs. Patterson's voice was patient and firm: "We got sixty-eight grandchildren and thirty-three great-grandchildren. We got a big generation." Mrs. Patterson smoothed her cotton apron. "It don't hurt nobody to tell what you think," she said, "I think there's a lot around here that'll write and try to get more added on their check. Some are getting $64 and up that away. We hain't. They claimed we drawed too much to get commodities. You ain't allowed to sell a calf unless you turn it in and they cut your check down. And we ain't got no way to get out of here to buy. I just shop around these little places—I call them peanut stores."

She said most of the young people are gone. "People have just quit lookin' for work around here and went off hunting for jobs. There ain't nothin' around here to work at. We got two children still live here on the creek. The rest scattered over the whole known world, 'peers like to me. Some in Clay County, some in Bell County, some in Dayton, some in Cleveland."

So Mrs. Patterson runs her four-room house for only her husband now, and they live in apparent mountain comfort on their old-age benefits. "We draw $55 apiece every month."

"We git some out of there," Frank said, waving toward the small garden just outside the paling fence. "I own, in all, sixty acres." There is coal under the land, but Frank, like most mountaineers, considers it a curse rather than a blessing. "There's plenty coal here," he said. There's a seven-foot vein. But most of the coal around here was sold out years ago. They sold mineral rights sixty years ago at least.

"Here we are sittin' on millions in coal, oil, and gas. They claim there's a pocket of oil and gas forty miles square in here. Over on Red Bird you can hear that gas a-squealin' before you get within half a mile of it. They struck oil, and it run just like water 'till they plugged it up.

"It don't do this country no good."

High in the air above Stinking Creek, a jet plane etched twin white lines across the blue sky. To Frank Patterson, it had something to do with a war in Vietnam. Sometimes at night he walks over to his son's house and listens to the radio. The war distresses most of the people on Stinking Creek because war means killing and suffering and sacrifice. And they know that war is evil.

The plane was soon gone, but the white lines remained sharp and straight in the windless sky. Frank Patterson squinted at the contrails for a long time.

"You can tell about everytime they have a battle," he said sadly. "Them planes go back here out of the east and you see them going and coming with those bumbs. They fly over to where they're making them bumbs in Tennessee. They got a big plant there, and they carry them bumbs out of there.

"I heard that President on the radio and the way he spoke; it grieved his heart to kill the women and little children."

A slender, wiry dark-haired boy, in his early teens, came into the yard with the long, loose stride of mountain boys. He came up on the porch, went directly to Mrs. Patterson, and mumbled something. He was one of the Pattersons' sixty-eight grandchildren.

Mrs. Patterson fumbled beneath the folds of her apron and produced a small cloth tobacco sack, rolled tightly and tied with a short length of string. She untied the string, unrolled the little sack, and fished a dollar from it. She handed the bill to the boy. He thrust the dollar into the pocket of his skin-tight denim jeans, and disappeared.

4 There Will Be a Reward

SPEED SIZEMORE WHISTLED softly at the pain as he broke the still-smoldering bits of coal in his bare hands and rearranged them in his shallow fireplace. He added a few cedar twigs. The spiraling blue-gray smoke increased in volume, but no flame appeared.

Speed and his wife, Rosa, had arrived home only minutes before, and the cabin had been empty and cold, with the coal fire dying for hours. They were still freezing from the treacherous climb up Pigeon Creek from its juncture with Stinking Creek. The snow, driven by a strong March wind, stings the face like bits of hurled fire when the departing winter winds vents their final wrath on Stinking Creek. Speed's one-room cabin, with its lean-to kitchen, provided shelter from the wind, but the chill had seeped in and claimed every dark corner. They huddled on creaking cane-bottomed straight chairs before the smoking coals, still bundled up against the cold, and hopefully watched the yet unfulfilled promise of the curling gray smoke: Speed in his black collarless overcoat and colorless hat, Rosa in her red sweater and blue cotton dress and apron, her head wrapped in a knotted scarf.

The silence was brief. Sixty-eight years of living on Stinking Creek have not killed Speed's zest for conversation. He rose, squinted out the twelve-inch-square pane of glass beside the fireplace, and said with a grin: "It's snowing pretty live. But I seen a new moon, so the weather'll change. It changes every time with a new moon."

He scowled at the reluctant fire and nodded to Rosa. "Pour on some coal oil." Rosa came to her feet obediently, fetched an old coffee can, and splashed a bit of its contents on the coals. Flames immediately filled the grate. "Git back," Speed told her. "It will flash on you."

The light from the fire pushed back the shadows and revealed a room crowded with two large beds and the accumulated treasures of forty-five

42

*Speed and Rosa Sizemore at home. The girl is
the granddaughter Kay Gambrel.*

years of married life on Pigeon Creek. Boxes, jars, paper bags, cartons, feed sacks, all filled and bulging with bits of cloth, buttons, used and re-straightened nails, medicine bottles, pins and needles; calendars with their lithographed scenes; one bed piled high with clothing, pieces of cloth, and stuffed boxes. The Sizemore wealth was all gathered in that one room.

Speed smiled from across the worn sandstone hearth and said with conviction "I'm glad you came. I like a feller that's friendly. Yes, man, I'm glad you came." Speed had issued the invitation a week earlier, down on Stinking Creek near the old blackened frame Erose School. "Come up, when you take a notion, and meet my old lady," Speed said.

Rosa, the "old lady," sat silently, chewing her tobacco and occasionally spitting discreetly at the fire. The burden of the conversation was upon Speed as man of the house, and he rose eagerly to the responsibility.

"I ain't even took off this ugly old coat," he said. And he chuckled. "Doggies! It's colder than thunder."

Rosa, a hint of offense in her voice, said, "I ain't cold." But she re-mained bundled and wrapped.

"There is nothing as contrary as a coal fire," Speed said. He poked at the blazing coals. Two emaciated kittens stalked defiantly to the hearth and began to settle before he fire. "Git," Speed said. The kittens appar-ently were familiar with the order and the consequence of noncompliance. They fled. "Them kittens been trying to die every day," Speed said.

Conversation with Speed is easy and sincere, and it offered the oppor-tunity to forget the bitterness and cold howling outside along the frozen banks of Pigeon Creek.

There was trouble in Vietnam, but Speed was unworried. "I been sittin' up 'til ten or eleven every night at my daughter's and listening to the talk on the radio. I heered President Johnson talk. He's a good man. He don't want nobody killed. He don't want no blood agin him when he dies."

Speed's own life has a familiar ring to anyone who has tarried long on Stinking Creek.

"I worked in the mines thirteen years and six months 'til I got hurt. I wish to the Lord I never had gone in a mine. I wouldn't have my back hurt for anything, but I was in a tight place and had some need for the money.

"Oh, I been bundled up plenty of times, but it ain't killed me yet. A clay bank fell on me oncet, and a wagon throwed me over a bank. But when the slate fell in the mine, that was the trick that done it. The slate falls—you don't hear it. It just comes down on you. Plenty of them men never get out when there's a big cave-in."

Rosa sat silently, but she managed an occasional smile to confirm what Speed was saying. Then she would lean forward, big hands folded in her lap, and spit toward the fire. The coals were hot now, and the spittle exploded into steam with the sound made by air brakes on large trucks.

"I can't dig. I can't chop," Speed said. "I can't lift nothin'. I can't garden. I can't do no man-work in this world."

But there was a distinct glow of warmth from the fire now, and it had a therapeutic effect on the spirit.

Speed patted Rosa affectionately. "I been married forty-five years," he said. And with mock righteousness: "Some don't keep 'em that long. A heap of fellows swap 'em, but I never did have that in mind. I don't guess I could eat after some of them." He and Rosa both giggled as he added, "My stomach's not too good nohow."

Speed winked. "Rosa don't give me no trouble. If I ever cussed her in my life, I don't remember nothing about it." Rosa snorted.

There was a clanking of the pull chain on the seasoned pine door of the lean-to kitchen, and a pretty brown-haired girl of thirteen came in. She was Kay Gambrel, a granddaughter of Speed and Rosa. Kay kept her tan jacket pulled tightly about her and settled near the fire. Melting snow glistened in her hair, and her dark eyes were filled with frank curiosity.

"This younger generation won't strike at a snake," Speed said. "They need to learn more. I see where I missed it. I went to part of the fourth grade and then I gave it up, and now I can't remember a single one of them dogged words. I take *Grit,* and my girl reads it to me."

Kay slipped out and returned with a piece of coal the size of a grapefruit. Speed placed it gently on the glowing coals and jabbed at it disapprovingly. "It's hard coal from a hard land. It just naturally don't want to catch."

Speed explained that Kay is "a girl of an orphan boy I raised. We raised one girl of our own and this boy, which was a boy of Rosa's when we got married.

"I raised the boy real good," Speed said. "I never hit him a lick."

"The boy" later confirmed, "Speed raised me good." His name is Linzy Gambrel, and Kay is one of his alert, dark-featured children. Linzy Gambrel is fifty-three and also lives with a back torn in a mine cave-in. His story:

"I spent twenty years in the coal mines; then the slate falls. You are shoveling coal, and it falls down and knocks the fire out of you. It hit me and knocked my back out of socket in two places."

Kay is less than enthusiastic about school. Do you like school? "Naw."
Do you have a favorite subject? "Naw."

"She does too," Speed said. "Yes, man, this is a good place to raise
kids. Some folks got the awfullest drove of youngsters you ever seen."

"That's the absolute truth," Rosa said, breaking her silence. She watched
to see if notes were to be taken on what she said, as on Speed's comments.
When she saw that her words were being recorded, she smiled approvingly.

"I'm seventy years old, and that's the truth, too," Rosa said.

Kay rose and stood by her grandmother. "I don't guess I'll ever see
that many years," she said. She was ready to leave. Linzy Gambrel sends
Kay up the creek on cold days to check on Speed and Rosa and to see
that the fire is burning and that there is no sickness. This duty performed,
Kay slipped quietly out into the gale and disappeared down the hollow.

Speed and Rosa, of course, live on welfare and social security. This
income from government bounty rises and falls, like the fortunes of all
mountain endeavors, depending upon the law, state and federal officeholders, social workers, and the skill and integrity of the recipient in seeking relief. Speed and Rosa generally stay above the $100-a-month level.

"They got no cause to cut the checks," Rosa said.

Speed agreed, "I don't believe that's no fair deal."

" 'Tain't, Rosa said firmly. "I was drawing $51 old age. They cut me
to $28, and I finally got it back to $36. She nodded toward Speed. "He
gets $19 on disability and $57 social security. A man can't get rich in
this country."

"I ought to have more than that," Speed agreed. "We got investigators
that don't want you to have anything. They just don't know your feelings."

Speed and Rosa don't qualify for surplus commodities. Speed said he
tried.

"The commodities? I wouldn't lie for it," Speed said. "I told two of
them, 'I declare now, you're two govermint men and what I'm telling you
I'll tell at Judgment. There's just the two of us at home. If I can't tell
the truth and get it, I'll just make out without it. I'll do the best I can.' "
He was turned down.

Speed looked at the fire awhile, then said, "If I starve, I'll just have to
starve."

"You ain't going to starve," Rosa said quickly, with a glance toward
the notebook.

"No, I guess I ain't," Speed said. "I got more faith than that."

Not entirely a religious faith.

"Me and the old woman don't go to preachin' much. Hardly got any, way out of here," Speed said. "But if you're wanting to hear some preachin', I'd recommend Preacher Marsee over on Buckeye Fork. We've got a need for more young people to go to preachin'. It will be a good blessing when they do. That preacher on Buckeye is good as they come. They got a store next door, and he won't let them go in that store during preachin'. People go into preachin' and don't leave until it breaks. They can go in the back door of the store if they're careful; but buddy, you better not let Preacher Marsee catch you at it during preachin'.

"Yes, man, you want to hear some preachin', I say hear Preacher Marsee. In my opinion, that one will satisfy you."

Gilbert Bargo also recommended Preacher Marsee, and Bargo is a man whose opinions merit respect.

Bargo's strength of character belies his slight build, his elfin appearance, his blue eyes pale from sixty-four years of squinting at the denuded hills that sweep upward from Stinking Creek. Bargo was swinging a heavy ax, shaping new runners for a sled. The sled is an invaluable conveyance to a hill farmer. Its heavy timber runners glide over rocks, mud, gravel, and dust, pulled along by a reluctant mule that can be driven to slopes no tractor can negotiate. A sled hauls wood for the winter fires, hay for the barn, stones from the fields—the countless heavy, bulky things that must be moved in the day-to-day labor of mountain farming.

When illness strikes far up a hollow, a sled is sometimes the only conveyance that can be used to transport the ailing person to a doctor. In the dead of winter, when creeks, which also serve as roadbeds, are frozen and the ground is covered with snow, a mule and a sled can reach the head of even the most remote hollow.

Sleds were used to haul coal down from the steeper grades, and old-timers say they used sleds to haul as much as two thousand pounds of tanbark at a time. "You'd cut a chestnut, oak, white oak, water oak for tanbark. Just skin it like you'd skin a cow, and then leave the logs to rot. Lots of good timber rotted up there on the hills in those days. They don't use tanbark anymore. That's why we don't get no good shoes anymore, no matter how dear we pay for them."

When the mule is pulling a heavily laden sled down a steep slope, the mountaineer uses a simple device to prevent the sled from overtaking the mule and crashing into its rear legs. This is the "rough lock," a length of chain secured to a front standard of the sled and allowed to drag under a runner. It acts as a brake, slowing the sled as it is brought down from the high places.

Bargo looks to the soil for his economic salvation rather than to the confusing array of welfare programs. His sled is vital to his future.

So on the first sunny day of the new year, Bargo climbed into the hills behind his house with his ax to seek timbers for sled runners. The runners must be strong and reliable, and the timber selected must curve correctly at the end so the grain will follow the upturned front edge of the runners and give them strength. Bargo selected one timber of ash and another of sourwood, each about eight inches in diameter, for the runners, felled them, and dragged them one at a time to the level place in front of his home by the creek. Then he selected a straight length of dogwood for the crosspiece, to which he will hitch the heavy pulling chains, and dragged it to where his worn sled lay waiting.

Bargo, swinging the ax with sure, deft strokes, peeled the bark from the logs and cut and shaped them into runners. With a large hand auger, he drilled the holes for the upright standards of the sled body, measuring carefully from the holes of the old, worn-out runners. When assembled, the new pieces fitted perfectly. Then Bargo, with short chopping strokes, trimmed the edges of the sled runners into shape.

He has lived on this farm for six years, and said modestly: "I claim 170 acres from that spur up there to the creek. "I've cleaned out the bottom. Had to dig out a grove of big sycamores and cut the roots as deep as I could. This was an old, throwed-away place when I come here six years ago. It takes a man a lot of time and expenses to get it in shape. I got that hillside plowed and worked now, and it won't wash down unless it comes a hard, dashing rain. I even got some fenceposts up there."

Bargo lives in a neat white clapboard house he built himself. "Maybe I hired out a hundred dollars' worth of work on it." He rested the ax blade on his heavy shoe to protect the keen edge, leaned against a fallen tree, and philosophized: "Naturally, this paper-poke living is pretty hard living, but it's all a man can do. If I had some pasture land I could live considerable better. A man living on a farm can't make a living without stock, and I ain't got no fences yet to speak of." But he has a start; you can see the pale-yellow peeled cedar fenceposts placed high on the hill behind his house. Bargo is improving his property as fast as he can.

But, "I still got four kids left in school, and that's some expense to cause a worry. They change the books too regular." His blue eyes crinkled and he laughed tolerantly at the foibles of educators. "They just change from one fool's ideas to another's. All this space and going around the world: they don't need to fool with that in the school."

So Bargo keeps his ax sharp and his bull-tongue plow free of rust so a

Gilbert Bargo

*Gilbert Bargo
repairing
his sled*

livelihood can be wrung from the thin, steep soil of his farm. He scoffs at "govermint business."

"These people they're helping, they could get by on their own. They could get to helping themselves. I see big fat hardy fellows drawing blind checks. If they can drive a car around and lead a dog around fox hunting, they ain't blind. The trouble is, and you know it as quick as I can tell you, some want it as a gift. They try every scheme in the world to get on some kind of aid. Fellows say to me, 'Go sign up and you'll get help without even tryin'.' But I never felt like sayin' something I couldn't back up. I'd rather live hard. Oh, I've been around them signin' up for commodities. Some'd tell how they didn't have nary a thing in the house, and I knowed better than that. Someday the govermint might get overloaded, and collapse."

After the sled was finished, Bargo hitched up his mule, loaded the sled with "barn litter," and began throwing the rotted manure and straw on his garden plot. Silently, the heavy pitchfork swung back and forth as Bargo hurled the litter in long sweeping motions. He broke the silence: "The Greeks did a smart thing when they started this." Those ancient agriculturists would agree with Bargo when he rubs a handful of gray dirt critically between his fingers and says quietly, "The ground can stand just so much."

Bargo's daily labors on the steep farm are exhausting, even for a much younger man, and this is not the life he wants for his children. His oldest son, Eugene, is twenty, and Bargo frequently asks whether one of the many government programs might hold out some hope for Eugene.

"This road thing [Appalachian bill], will it employ many?" he asked. Turning to "govermint" aid is embarrassing for Bargo. Eugene "went through the eighth grade," and Bargo knows the boy's chances of breaking away from the cycle of hardship are slim. "The trouble with the road work is, you have to have some practice with machinery," he said, and there was a note of finality in his voice. "And timbering is no good. This country has had a terrible lot of timber, but it's getting scarce."

There seems no way out for the boy—except to follow in his father's footsteps up and down the stubborn rows of the hillside farm. But the boy, like most boys on Stinking Creek, has no desire to turn to the rocky soil. While his father coaxes his fields from early morning to sundown, the boy sits on the front porch or sometimes tinkers on an ancient automobile with a friend, and waits for a suitable opportunity to present itself.

Bargo also has seven daughters still at home, ranging from ten-year-old Dorothy Jean to thirty-two-year-old Eselene. The Bargo front porch usually is alive with this array of feminine offspring, and a wave from a passing car sets off a flurry of slender hands. The Bargo girls are quiet, and do little "courtin'." With their mother, they attend church, elections, and other Stinking Creek functions in a group, sticking closely together. Two other boys and a girl have married and gone. Of the eight children at home, Bargo says, "It makes a hard life for them."

Bargo leaned for a minute on his pitchfork, and said: "So much of this, that and t'other; so much one season, so much another season; it keeps me in a press. One fellow said to me he don't see how I do what I do with this place. Well, it ain't the strength; it's the willingness you got."

Bargo's willingness comes partly from the inspiration he gets "over at the mouth of Buckeye Fork." That is where the Salem Baptist Church sits and that is where Preacher Marsee preaches. And Bargo confirmed Speed Sizemore's opinion of Preacher Marsee "As good a preaching as you'd ever care to hear."

On the following Sunday morning, Bargo walked the mile or so up the muddy creek road to the Salem Baptist Church at the mouth of Buckeye Fork. He had cleaned his high-top shoes, the collar of his plaid shirt was buttoned neatly at his neck; his overalls were freshly washed; and he wore his brown hat with its turned-up brim squared away an inch above his pale-blue eyes. His wool suitcoat was buttoned.

Salem Baptist Church is a wooden building, about thirty-six feet long and twenty-four feet wide. Its sturdy pews are varnished and shiny, and so is its pulpit, worn but still sound despite years of fist banging by visiting preachers. Four bare bulbs hang in the ceiling to light the interior. Behind the pulpit, a large banner declares "Welcome." Also behind the pulpit are pictures of Christ, including two that adorn large calendars advertising funeral homes. An occasional nail driven into the wall accommodates the hats and coats of early arrivals.

A choir composed of half a dozen men and as many teen-aged boys and girls opened the service. Clustered behind the pulpit, they sang the old favorites "Have a Little Talk with Jesus" and "Rock of Ages."

There were sixty-two people in the church: old men, young men, youths, babies, women with men and women without men. A fervor filled the room, and there were humming and tapping of feet, and voices began to join the singing. The choir sang from well-used paperback hymnals, the others from memory.

The singing voices in Salem Baptist Church are strong, untrained, sincere, and convincing. The words echoed in the small building.

Salem Baptist Church

"When my journey is completed and there is no more work to do . . ."

A group of teen-aged boys came hurriedly in the door and settled on a back pew.

"Savior, guide my weary spirit . . ."

A dark-brown upright piano stood silently in the corner, its top decorated with a bowl of artificial fernlike plants in fading pastel colors. Nobody in the congregation plays the piano.

"When the storm around me rages . . ."

One window had been broken, but a piece of cardboard cut from a breakfast cereal carton kept out the cold.

"Rock of Ages, hide thou me . . ."

Then prayers, a rustle of voices that began quietly throughout the building, rose and faded, blended and contrasted, with supplication, confession, and thanksgiving. It was a surging, fervent sound that filled the church and was neither of ecstasy nor of torment, but a broad, sweeping wave of emotion torn between those two extremes of human feeling.

Then a collection. One by one, members of the congregation rose, walked forward, and laid money on the pulpit. Gilbert Bargo rose at length, smoothed and counted the bills, stacked the change, and solemnly announced, "I want to thank the congregation for $15.30 for the preacher." Bargo is the official church clerk.

Then the man recommended by both Speed Sizemore, who never hears him, and by Gilbert Bargo, who often does, stepped to the pulpit.

The Reverend A. S. Marsee, an erect, gray-haired man of sixty-five, slender and confident, was meticulously dressed in a dark suit, white shirt, the only necktie in the room, and black polished shoes. Preacher Marsee was a man in command; an erect man, fitting and proper in dress and bearing to incur the favor of the most sophisticated congregation. But he quickly dispelled that illusion. Preacher Marsee had come to confront evil on Stinking Creek—and offer an eternal salvation—and he preached with a simple strength that was both jolting and refreshing.

Preacher Marsee removed his tie with the first words of his sermon, folded it neatly, and deposited it somewhere beneath the podium.

"You're going to want something that will not fail you," he said. "Brother, if you had diamonds as large as the state of Kentucky and precious stones stacked to the sky, if you had them in your dying hour, you would give them to know what's awaitin' you on the other side."

His voice was strong and pitched high. He plunged directly into his message, his slender blue-veined hands alternately crashing down on the unyielding podium and sweeping high above his head.

"The things man has done has failed.

"Temple worship has failed."

Preacher Marsee forced each shouted sentence from his throat with an audible gasp of the last bit of breath remaining in his lungs. The gasps punctuated and emphasized them. And each one followed on the heels of the preceding sentence like a demon in pursuit of a soul.

"Adam failed. Huh. He failed miserable. Huh.

"And Noah failed. Huh. Jacob failed. Huh. And Moses and Solomon. Huh. These were great men, but they went down under the blows of Satan, Huh.

"God's favored race has not produced one man who is a match for the Devil. Huh. Not one man or woman in this world is a match for the Devil. Huh."

There was a rhythmic, hypnotic flow to Preacher Marsee's delivery, and his congregation sat transfixed. He leaned far out over the podium, pointed a slender forefinger toward the floor, and cried, "Even David, the great warrior. All these men went down. Huh."

Briefly, there was silence, except for a faint spewing of the coal fire in the cast-iron stove that squats in front of the pulpit.

But Preacher Marsee had not come to deal with the ancient past. He removed his coat, folded it, and laid it beneath the pulpit. Preacher Marsee had come to deal with evil on Stinking Creek, and he turned eagerly to the business at hand.

"Oh, my God, if an atomic bomb fell this morning, the only safe hiding place is in Jesus Christ. Huh. He would not fail, brother. Huh."

In the congregation, a voice agreed, "Never."

"I could call witness after witness. Huh. A woman touched His hem. He didn't fail. Huh. I could call the leper. Huh. I could call the blind man. Huh."

Preacher Marsee began to precede an occasional sentence with a short, shrill cry of exultation.

"Whooo! When He came out of the tomb, He came to man the lifeboat of salvation. Huh. And there is room in that boat for you, brother. God gave you a ticket. Huh. I'll preach what I'm preaching here anywhere. I'll preach it to kings and queens. You take that man on that hill with a bull-tongue plow. Huh. I'll preach it to him. Huh. I'll preach it in every cabin on that mountain. Huh. He said, 'I give eternal life and thou shalt never perish.' Huh."

A deep voice in the congregation agreed, "Never."

"He said, 'Upon this rock I'll build my church and it will not fail,'

Preacher
A. S. Marsee

brother. Huh. A century after Isaiah wrote this message, there comes the Lord, Jesus Christ. Huh. That church started with twelve men, and what a struggle they had. Huh. But, my God, that was Christ's church. Whooo! And today, brother, there are millions of people. Huh. There are people right here today that would die for it. Whooo! We'll let every drop of blood run out of our body before we'll give up our church. Huh."

On Stinking Creek, as on a thousand creeks in a thousand hollows, there can be no rewards here on earth. All that promised has failed. The virginal forests have become a wasteland. The richness of coal has left poverty. Only floods, sickness, ignorance, and agony can find their way down the gurgling, polluted streams. The paradise the Long Hunter found has become a prison for his descendants. Everyone on Stinking Creek knows that. Preacher Marse knows it. Gilbert Bargo knew it as he sat erectly on the front pew, his calloused hands clutching each other as he strained to share in the salvation Preacher Marsee offered. And Preacher Marsee gladly offered what he did have to offer—a paradise somewhere in another life.

Preacher Marsee moved from the pulpit and stood, a straight, confident figure in shirt sleeves, among the pews, his face pink with exertion. His voice dropped to a soft, fatherly tone.

"We fail many ways in this world," he said. "We may limp through life. A doctor can lose a patient. A farmer can lose a crop. But the Great Shepherd never loses a sheep."

Then Preacher Marsee came back to the podium, struck it a resounding blow with his hand, and his voice climbed back to its preaching pitch eagerly and triumphantly:

"I don't want a religion I have to guess about. Huh. I want the one that's salvation. I want the one that stood the fiery furnace. Huh. I want the one that let Daniel sleep on that lion's mane. Huh. That same power is here today. Huh. That old-time religion. Whooo! I'm interested in eternity, brother, and I'm going to be there. Huh. I'm on that rock. Huh."

Preacher Marsee preached for nearly an hour, giving no quarter, asking none. It was his moment of truth with the forces of evil on Stinking Creek, and he meant to leave a message that would last two weeks. Salem Baptist Church holds services on the first and third Sundays of each month. He made no apology for keeping the enthralled congregation. Instead, he waved an invisible banner high in his right hand and cried:

"A woman told me once, 'Preacher, you preached too long.' She said I let her roast burn. Well, brother, it's better to let things burn here than in eternity."

Preacher Marsee knew there was a stranger in the congregation. He turned his clear boring blue eyes, lifted his Bible, and said: "I'm not preaching to get in a book. I'm preaching from a Book." He was nearing the end of his sermon, and wanted all his cards on the table. "When you lose your sins, it'll be a breathless moment in eternity. Don't miss heaven. Trust Christ." Three strides took him back to the center of the church, and he closed, "How many of you will say, 'Preacher, I want that'?"

Salem Baptist Church had got its $15.30 worth of preaching. The congregation flocked to Preacher Marsee, shaking hands vigorously, with an occasional "God bless you," an occasional sob.

Everyone filed outside, big calloused hands extended in "Christian brotherhood." Invitations that were not invitations, but only acknowledgments of acceptance, "You better come to dinner."

Snow had begun to fall, large wet flakes that floated down gently like a benediction. Gilbert Bargo returned home in silence. "Preaching does a heap of good," he said softly.

If Preacher Marsee is reluctant to promise the people of Stinking Creek "diamonds as large as the state of Kentucky" and a literal paradise here on earth, there are others who are willing.

Two days after Preacher Marsee's sermon, there was a distinguished gathering in the rose garden of the White House in Washington. The President was there to sign a piece of legislation, and in attendance were smiling governors, congressmen, and federal and state officials.

The President's name was Johnson, and he was once poor himself. Among the chief executives of the eleven Appalachian states, one governor in particular was known, by name at least, on Stinking Creek. His name is Breathitt. He has never been especially poor.

The Washington weather was mild and the assemblage impressive. It was fitting that it be so. The bill the President signed was called the Appalachia Act, and it boldly holds out a hope of—if not paradise exactly —something better than what has been known in hollows throughout the mountains, including Stinking Creek.

It is good that the President did not hear Preacher Marsee. He might have found the sermon disquieting. The President himself, sitting at the center of attention in the sun-dappled rose garden, was optimistic. He called the bill "the truest example of creative federalism of our times," and said, "It marks the end of an era of partisan cynicism toward human want." He also said that the stroke of his pen had just signaled that the era "of the pork barrel is gone."

The governors smiled. The congressmen smiled. The state and federal officeholders smiled. They are all going to help spend the more than one billion dollars that will put a little of paradise back into Stinking Creek. Most of the money is going to be used to build roads—superhighways that will lace across the groaning mountains. Perhaps they will bring prosperity and joy.

The mountains have long memories. Many times before there have been cries of Utopia. Wild expectations came with the first Long Hunters from the Carolinas and Virginia, who rubbed their eyes in disbelief at the lush forests, the crystal streams, the abundance of wildlife.

There was joy when the coal industry boomed. Thousands of men went into the mountains to earn fabulous wages. The economy soared beyond their wildest dreams, and men squandered their wealth at the coal company stores on silk shirts and fifty-cent cigars.

And half a century ago the railroads came slashing through the mountains. Appalachia was united with the world, and there would be no more isolation, no more want, no more hunger—ever.

Strangely, there was no celebration on Stinking Creek on that March day when the President signed the Appalachia Act.

At Mills, Kentucky, the tiny one-room post office stands impassively near the rocky spot where Acorn Fork gurgles into Stinking Creek. An American flag fluttered wearily in the breeze to remind the citizens that they were dealing with federal authority.

An old man, tailed by a sullen beagle dog, came up the road from the post office, leaning slightly into the wind. The old man dug thoughtfully at a piece of dried brown tobacco juice clinging to the graying hairs of his unshaven chin, and offered a comment on the Appalachia Act.

"Muleshit," he said.

5 Browns Hollow

CORDIE BROWN BROUGHT her sow down from the head of Browns Hollow to be bred on a sultry, dusty day in midsummer. The dark thunderclouds building over the mountains to the west were once again promising rain, but all the Browns knew better than to believe. Each day the clouds would gather and darken, but then they would move around the mountain to the north and west, leaving Browns Hollow bone dry and white with dust from the parched banks of the creek. All that remained of Browns Branch itself was a dismal trickle along a sandstone bed, now fed only by a stubborn spring far up the hollow.

Browns Branch, where all the Browns live, is not far from Stinking Creek. A few miles above its mouth at the Cumberland River, Stinking Creek bends eastward into a large hollow. At that point it is joined by Middle Fork, one of its principal tributaries. Two miles or so up Middle Fork, twin hollows jut out on either side like crooked arms. To the right, Johns Branch runs in; to the left, Browns Branch enters.

It is at this junction that Rosie Brown lives alone. Hard by the bank of Johns Branch, she has built a sturdy pigpen of stout saplings woven together with heavy rusty wire. In the pen is Rosie's boar, a squat, irritable beast that provides a substantial part of Rosie's income. His breeding fee is two dollars, and Cordie and Rosie agreed amiably on this price.

In a sense, Cordie and Rosie are kindred souls. Rosie's man is gone, and Cordie is raising her brood of seven boys far up Browns Hollow without the complications of a husband. Cordie is forty-two, plump and jolly. With her boys, she farms the level patches of her place, raises pigs and chickens, and leads a full life. Her garden is generous and her cow is willing. Rosie, some twenty years older, is larger. A strong, sincere woman, her clear blue-gray eyes are friendly. She gardens one of the biggest bottoms on Johns Branch, unawed by the swarms of natural-born Browns

Browns Hollow

around her. Rosie is a Brown by marriage, but Floyd Brown is a jovial dreamer; and after some forty-two years of wedded bliss at the mouth of Browns Branch, Floyd rolled his spare trousers into a bundle, stuck them under his arm, and moved into a weathered house about ten yards away. Floyd and Rosie are the best of neighbors, and their nearness is convenient when the two boys and five girls they raised come to visit. Floyd is convinced he will never move back in with Rosie.

"I ain't through lookin' around yit," he said.

Cordie showed up at the mouth of Johns Branch around noon on the appointed day. Her blue pickup truck was brimming with some of her boys, other assorted Brown small fry, Charley Brown, Cordie's older brother who came along to help, and the sow. Cordie wheeled the truck onto the nearly dry bed of Johns Branch, and Charley and the boys secured the sow with a length of rope, fought her into the pen with the boar, and tied her securely to the sapling fence.

Charley remained by the pen to oversee the consummation of the transaction; the boys repaired to a nearby abandoned truck flat bed to watch. The crowd of boys were joined there by Henry Brown, the eighty-one-year-old head of the Brown clan. Henry, who represents the accumulated wisdom of the Browns, sat on the edge of the truck bed puffing his pipe. He removed his brown corduroy cap to let whatever breezes that might stray that way cool his thick gray hair, now matted with perspiration. The boys squatted and watched patiently in the manner of mountain men.

Mountain men rarely sit. They squat, a habit adopted by their forebears from the Indians generations ago. They can squat for hours, their buttocks an inch from he dusty ground, the knees inches from the face. Squatting must be learned early. It is impossible for the uninitiated to squat and talk with a mountain man. After a few minutes, the thigh muscles scream in agony and the hips cramp with a fiery pain. The boys squatted on the rotted truck bed patiently, perfectly balanced, unmoving except for an occasional slight turn of the head to send a stream of dark-brown tobacco juice arching into the dust.

Spitting is no less an art than squatting. From the small boys and girls to the ancient, ageless old-timers, nearly everybody on Stinking Creek spits constantly. The very young emit a pristine, clear spittle innocent of tobacco. At about the age of ten or eleven, tobacco adds its color to the flying globs, each propelled with a quick, expert contraction of the cheek and tongue muscles. In winter they spit at the fireplace. In summer, they spit with no apparent target. A mother nursing a baby can send a stream of the

Henry Brown

brown fluid sailing out through an open door six feet away without getting a drop on her, the baby, or the doorstoop.

During a conversation, the spitter keeps his eyes fixed politely on you, turns his head almost imperceptibly, and spits—sometimes into the wind, sometimes downwind. Their accuracy is phenomenal, and no one on Stinking Creek is ever spat upon.

The mating of swine is not an inspirational performance. It is not by oversight that poets ignore the crude antics of swine and devote their talents to the more suitable arenas of butterflies and rabbits. Swine come to their nuptial couch with unclean hocks, clumsily and with revolting tenacity.

Cordie and Rosie retired discreetly to Rosie's front porch and left the witnessing of the breeding to Henry, Charley, and the boys. This audience was, at first, silent and inquisitive. But at length the boys began to chide Henry, careful to keep a respectful tone in their voices.

"That boar's like an old man, ain't he, Henry?"

Henry let a smile twitch at the corners of his thin lips, and replied, "I'd a been on her three times by now."

A small boy came to Henry's defense: "Henry'd have her topped and gone by now."

The boys kept their eyes on the pen and gently goaded Henry to see how far they could go, knowing that the first stern word from the spokesman of the Brown clan would command absolute silence. But Henry was caught up in the festive mood of the occasion.

"It's bad you gettin' excited over that, Henry."

"It don't bother me none."

"Buddy, you put me in that pen and bring me a woman and I wouldn't charge no two dollars. Would you, Henry?"

"What you boys got to understand is that Rosie's got that boar to feed. It may be two months before anybody brings another sow to him," Henry said.

There was a silence, all eyes on the pen, until a spindly boy, his voice still pitched high with adolescence, shifted his weight nervously and blurted: "He's done fucked that sow half to death. How much does Cordie want for her two dollars?"

There was a ripple of chuckling from the other boys that brought a blush of embarrassment to the outspoken youth's face. Henry, removing the pipe from his mouth and clearing his throat, came to his defense. The boys turned to him with respect and inquisitiveness. When Henry has something to say, you can usually learn something.

"Once is all it takes," Henry said. "Time I brought a sow over to Carnses' boar, he jumped her once, and they said, 'Get that sow out.' One time's good as a dozen. That sow brought seven of the prettiest pigs I ever saw. One shot. One good lick is all you need."

The boys listened fascinated. Henry, in eighty-one years of living and raising eight separate families, has acquired a storehouse of practical knowledge. The boys squatted quietly, their eyes urging Henry to continue. He relit his pipe, and asked, "You know how many germs in a bull?"

Silence.

"One hundred and sixty in one lick."

The impromptu lecture on biology was not yet finished. Henry had one last fact of life to toss at the boys.

"You boys know the difference between a man and a woman?"

Heads shook slowly in a negative answer.

"Well, sir, a woman's always ready, and a man's got to git ready."

Charley Brown interrupted the session. From his vantage point by the pen he called out, "Let's get her out of here." That was the signal for Cordie to come over from Rosie's porch and for the boys to leap to the pen to manhandle the sow back into the pickup truck. The sow was loath to leave. Squealing, screaming, protesting, she dug her sharp hooves into the dirt and defied the efforts of the assembled Browns. The Browns, with Cordie helping, pulled, pushed, fought, and forced the sow toward the truck. Once she broke away and dashed back toward the pen.

The struggle was repeated in a cloud of gray dust kicked up by the laboring Browns. A youth slipped and fell to his knees. He seized a hammer and screamed, "Git in that truck you damned sow or I'll give you some of this hammer!"

The sow safely loaded, Cordie climbed in behind the wheel, the boys clambered into the back with the still-protesting sow, and the bumpy journey back up Browns Hollow began.

Henry remained behind, sitting on the edge of the old truck bed and puffing thoughtfully on his pipe. He stared at the pigpen, and at length the boar stuck his snout out between the saplings and stared back at Henry. The old man and the boar regarded each other solemnly.

When his pipe was burned out, Henry banged it on the truck bed to shake loose the ashes, blew into it, and filed it away carefully in a pocket of his overalls. Henry picked up his hickory cane, rapped it on the ground twice to test its soundness, and broke the silence.

"Gettin' critters borned is mighty important, in my opinion."

He turned, walked out into the sun, and started slowly up the creek bank toward Browns Hollow.

At the mouth of Browns Hollow, an old man holding two yellow lard cans filled with freshly picked blackberries stood at the edge of the narrow road. He pondered the question:

"Is everybody in this hollow named Brown?"

The old man, a lean, graying mountaineer, leaned nearer. His answer was deliberate and firm: "They better be."

If there is a wrong side of the tracks on Stinking Creek, it is Browns Hollow. Behind Rosie Brown's house and boar pen, at the junction of Brown Branch and Middle Fork, a steep, almost impassable road climbs between narrowing walls of towering mountains. The passage writhes between huge boulders that over the centuries have tumbled down the mountains to rest on the floor of Browns Hollow. Along this valley live the Browns.

In Barbourville, where many social and political leaders have never seen the upper reaches of Browns Hollow, they warn: "Don't go up Browns Hollow. Outsider like you don't know what they're getting into. Those Browns are a peculiar outfit. Don't have a thing to do with nobody in this world. Just drink and stick to themselves. Even marry each other."

The Browns are misunderstood.

Henry Brown, the spokesman of the clan who had presided at the mating of the swine, was sitting at a vantage point on his front porch. The house is perched on a high place, and from his porch Henry can sit and rock and observe the goings and comings far up and down the hollow. Friendly and quiet, with the serene air of a man in command, Henry wears steel-rimmed glasses that frame clear blue eyes which crinkle at the corners. He dresses in fading Washington Dee Cee overalls, the bib extending up over a yellow shirt, and brown shoes. His long hands, purple and brown, are splotched with age. Facing the narrow road are the houses of his brothers, Dewey and Daw; his cousins, Bowman and Charley Brown, and dozens of other Browns up and down the hollow.

"I guess I'm sort of the head of the Brown family," Henry said. "I tell them the best that I know what to do." His cool eyes measured; he searched out the meaning of questions, weighing their intent. Henry Brown, the horse trader, spokesman for a family, polite, unhurried, at last decided:

"Come on up on the porch, brother. You're welcome to stay with the Browns 'til you starve out."

How came the Browns to this scenic, isolated fold in the mountains? What holds them here? The Browns present a genealogical Gordian knot. Once, Henry eagerly helped in an attempt to draw a chart tracing the Brown family tree. It ended in frustration. Henry, however, found it fascinating, and would have continued the project for weeks, but at last could say only, "There's quite a drove of us, brother."

Before the Civil War, a huge man from the Carolinas walked up the untamed reaches of Middle Fork. At a small tributary, he turned west, following the creek to near its source. The hollow was alive with bear, deer, and small game. The big man stood at length on a level place and looked around. He slept there, and in the morning he put aside his heavy rifle and his grubbing hoe, took up his ax, and began to build a cabin.

No human being was around to hear the biting of Steve Brown's ax into the virgin forests. In time, he married a frontier girl named Thursday Ann Bingham. Steve Brown hunted, raised tobacco, squash, beans, and corn and gradually increased the cleared area around his cabin. In time, Thursday Ann bore him five sons and four daughters. Long before the last child was born, hunters who infrequently came that way were calling the lush dimple in the mountain Browns Hollow. The stream that gushed along the hollow was called Browns Branch.

Two of the sons born in that hollow were named Melvin and Henry, and they stayed in Browns Hollow to cut the timbers, labor in the steep fields, and live the independent, hard life their father led.

Melvin Brown had a daughter named Cordie, who still lives high in the hollow with her seven sons and fertile sow; and two sons, Bowman and Charley, who also live in the hollow today.

Henry Brown, the son of the man who found Browns Hollow, also built a cabin, married, and had twelve children. One of his sons he named Henry, after himself. This is the man who now, at eighty-one, speaks for the Browns. Daw and Dewey Brown are his brothers, and they, too, live with their big families in Browns Hollow.

These are the direct descendants of "old man Steve." But from there, the lines cross and entangle; they disappear into outside bloodlines, and abruptly reappear.

"Daw married Melvin's girl Pearly."

"Charley married my sister Dora's girl Cleo."

At one house, just around a huge boulder that threatens to shut off access to the upper part of the hollow, the surname is Collins. But Bill Collins, awash in a sea of Browns, is entrenched in the family hierarchy.

"Bill Collins married Melvin's girl."

Henry Brown, his eighth woman, and his family

Dewey Brown's family

"Dewey Brown, Junior, married Bill Collins' girl Jacqueline."

"Henry's girl married Bill Collins' boy Curtis."

What of Floyd and Rosie Brown, once married but now living side by side down at the mouth of the creek?

"Well, that's another set of Browns, sort of. Floyd's daddy was a George Brown. Fred and L. C. are his boys. I think some of their kin somewhere was Nortons."

And one of the Browns up the hollow said of the Browns down at the mouth of the creek, "Durn if I know where they terminated from."

There was a time when the Browns lived by hunting, farming, logging, and occasionally brewing "a drap or two" of moonshine. The only thriving industry in Browns Hollow now is welfare. It keeps the Browns alive.

Commodities and welfare checks pour into Browns Hollow to replace the timber that is gone, the game that is gone, and the topsoil that long ago was flushed down the creek.

Henry Brown counted up one day and decided there were ninety-six Browns living along the little creek, from Steve, named for the man who started the clan and living in the last house up the hollow, to Louis, who lives down where the hollow widens into a flat bottom, and ends. On a dry day, when the creek is not up over the road too far, you can walk from Louis's house to Steve's in about half an hour, past all the Browns.

Henry insists his health is failing, but almost daily he walks spryly down the rough road, jabbing his cane at the stones, and out to the paved road that follows Middle Fork. He does all the family "trading" at the small stores, and on occasion can be found in Barbourville, twenty miles from his house, arguing politics or watching the cattle sell under the auctioneer's chant at the stockyards.

Barbourville has become a shameful place for the hill leaders such as Henry Brown to gather. When the new courthouse was built, no room was left for the rows of benches that traditionally grace Kentucky courthouse lawns. So the elderly men, dispossessed, gather uncomfortably in knots across the street from the unfriendly building and sit on the stoops of the stores.

"My legs have give way and my eyes water so bad I can't see," Henry complains. But he can identify a mule several hundred yards down the road from his porch. "From my knees to my neck I'm sound as a dollar. Feel like I'm sixteen in all that part of my body. But my heads stays stopped up. I had a notion to go to Lexington and see one of them head specials. These doctors here know very little more than I do. One wanted to experiment on one of my girls. I said, 'You experiment on one of your own girls, you want to experiment.' "

Henry prefers to treat himself, whenever the ailment doesn't threaten to become fatal.

"There's a heap of good healing stuff right here on this mountain. There ain't a weed on this globe but what's a benefit if you know where to put it." He pointed a veined finger toward the slope behind his house. "Right thar's a ragweed. You could be running off at your bowels. Nothing but water. You bile down those ragweed tops and make a tea. Drink half a cup. It'll stop. Blackberry roots do the same thing. A bowel complaint on anybody is well right off."

He paused to light his pipe.

"Hit's a weed around here—we call it niggerweed or sometimes iron blood. Dig the roots. It makes your iron blood. If you ain't got enough iron blood and get run down, you may have enough of the other blood but no iron blood. Brother, this niggerweed will put it in you. And swamp root. It's good fer different things. Bile it down into a strong tea, and there stands the prettiest blue oil on top of that water you ever saw. It's good for your kidneys. Bile it down good and strong."

Henry can't remember being seriously ill, but age has changed his eating habits.

"I tell you what I always wanted to eat—a big bowl full of clear grease and some biscuits. That was my main eatin'. But now I can't eat no breakfast. Now, the biggest thing I live on is milk. I got a good cow. She's a four-year-old blocky cow. I wouldn't sell her for no kind of money."

Eating, in most of the homes in the hollows that branch out from Stinking Creek, is a somber, serious business. In homes where poverty is kept at bay, there are laughter, even grace said by a child—and cleanliness. But in many homes the mother wearily announces, "I reckon it's ready."

You shuffle in, eat quietly, eyes down. Actually, there is usually plenty. Fresh green beans, corn, squash, and cucumbers in the summer. Always the cheese, peanut butter, and rice from the commodity program. Or commodity meat—chicken, beef, pork—fried in a heavy iron skillet. Dishes with a film, partly from the iron precipitate in the wash water, partly from lack of soap. Dishes with deep ancient cracks harboring something dark and just out of reach. Strong "biled" coffee.

Eat silently. Eating is not for fun, but to stay alive. Children, big eyes peering curiously, reach into their plates like robots. Pick up. Chew. Swallow. Look at Mother. Another spoonful from the big bowl in the

L. C. Brown's children

center of the table. Again. Pick up. Chew. Swallow. Run when you're filled.

Four hours later, a weary announcement: "I reckon it's ready."

Pinto beans, soaked and boiled with a piece of white "side meat." Boiled potatoes. Big tasteless biscuits. Strong "biled" coffee. Filling. Unsatisfying. Something to be gotten over with.

When Henry Brown was younger and starting each day with a bowl of clear grease, he was quite a man. All the Browns confirm this.

"When I was a boy I split old tough oak rails, and I could split two hundred in a day. I got fifty cents a hundred. Oncet I got a quarter for hoeing corn all day 'til suppertime. I was jest a boy and I hoed my rows and hope the men hoe theirs. But the man we was working for gave the men fifty cents and me a quarter. And I hoed twice as much as they did. But I didn't say nothing. Took the quarter.

"And I hope my daddy cut yellow poplar logs twenty-eight and thirty inches wide, and rolled them up in a big log pile and burned them. Twenty-five or thirty men could clear out a mountain in a day or two. Used them big crosscut saws for two men. All that just to make a little corn."

Young Henry Brown also kept tab on the mountain ladies in most of the nearby hollows.

"I used to play the gitar, fiddle and banjo. I don't play no more, but I used to be good, brother. Yeah, I've had my part of women. Started when I was seventeen. Women liked me. Never had no trouble gettin' any I wanted. This woman I got right here is my eighth woman. My women and me, I'd say all the young uns we've had around my house would be about twenty-one. We had seven or eight young uns get up to be big fellows just die. One of my women and me lost five or six. Great big chaps. Just get sick and die."

Henry has six children at home, from seven-year-old Stoney to Wanda Lee, who is twenty. "And I got four kids in Deetroit. Wouldn't stay here 'tall. I got a daughter in Deetroit in a $15,000 house."

Henry says the children in Detroit constantly ask him to visit. But he wants no part of the city. He prefers the hollow where he was born, has lived all his full life, and where he plans to die.

He said, a tone of reverence in his voice, "I don't guess there's a rock in this holler I ain't spit on."

Nearly every time Henry Brown looks up into the familiar mountains, he is reminded of a boyhood escapade. "There's a big hole in that mountain, and when I was a boy I would carry rocks up in my pockets and

Judy Ann Brown

Lilly Mae Brown

Quillie Brown

throw them in that hole. It was a granddaddy hole. You could hear them rocks drap . . . and drap . . . and drap . . . 'bout long as I been talkin' about it. And then they'd hit water."

Of his education: "I went to school all the time I was school age. I never went into arithmetic in my life, but there ain't a man here can beat me figurin'. Did my reading in an old McGuffey speller and a blue-back Webster."

Henry held up an index finger and with the index finger of his other hand marked off about two inches. "Had words that long. You never went in no grade then. You just went 'til you quit. I went 'til I was about sixteen or seventeen, and didn't have no books. A teacher learned me on a blackboard. I walked all the way down there with the frost bucking up between my toes."

As Browns Hollow goes, Henry Brown is well endowed with worldly goods. He has a potato hole to store his winter potatoes, two level garden plots, a barn, "that cow, a black pony, and a big mule." He manipulates his financial affairs to keep this agricultural establishment going.

"When I got to buy hay it's fifty cents to $1.25 a bale. They get $3.25 for shelled corn. That's pretty high, brother, for just a bushel and about three pecks."

Henry receives $87 a month welfare "for the children," and $60 a month social security. When a check comes, he usually owes at least half of it at the tiny rural groceries and in Barbourville stores for clothing or hardware.

"You might say we stay in debt . . . head over heels. Sometimes it's for feed stuff—corn, hay. Or shoes. I got good credit everywhere. I run a credit at Hubbard's. I can get credit. I got a good credit. I got no money in the bank. I buy a lot of shoes and pay high for 'em, brother. I buy my young uns three, four pairs before school's out."

Henry cashed his welfare check in a tiny store the next day. He owed $30. The proprietor deducted this amount and counted out the balance, placing the money in Henry's steady, outstretched palm. Henry put the money away in his pocket and sat silently on an upturned soft-drink case. The proprietor waited. Finally, Henry said, "Reckon I'll do some trading."

Henry is a wise shopper. He bought meal, flour, lard, coffee, bread, dried beans, salt pork, sugar. It came to $23. Henry gathered it all into a neat stack, and said, "Put it on the credit."

The rising cost of living bothers Henry. It is difficult to convince the welfare people that the checks should increase correspondingly. "I was down at Hubbard's store, and they said pinto beans was costing $20 a hundred wholesale. I got to buy them for the family. I don't like beans or Irish potatoes. I eat a egg every now and then and a little meat and milk. I can't stand sweetenin'. I just want a good fat piece of meat."

Although no formal family records are kept, and much of the Brown lore is lost, there is a deep feeling of family unity, as outsiders have discovered when they come "to give trouble."

"Had some fellers crawl out of this holler pretty busted up."

The Browns, particularly the younger men, may crack a bottle on a Saturday night, and wild shots have been known to shatter the quiet, but any Brown will tell you, as Henry does: "Almost all Browns is civil people and bother nobody without somebody bothers them. Just the ones that marry in causes trouble usually. Browns always done their duty."

Henry disappeared into another room and came back with a heavy sawed-off firearm.

"Hit's a musket my daddy had. Hit was used by Browns when they fit the Revolution War. They whipped them Englishmen. This musket was sawed off about four feet to make a boy a rabbit gun. Them old flintlocks had a pan, and the hammer hit that pan with the flint. Them was good shootin' guns."

Although the Browns dip heavily into a largess for which the Democratic Party receives primary credit, they are solidly Republican. There is a reason for this, Henry explained:

"It has to do with the slavery. They was slaves in Knox County. I knowed one—went by the name of Nigger Ned. He was bought as a suckling baby for $500. Nigger Ned worked all of his life, and finally the man said, 'Ned, I'm gonna set you free.' Ned was old and useless, and he just wandered around like a lost soul. He couldn't work no more, and he would come up and he'd be welcome to a bite of eat.

"When Nigger Ned died, they buried him by a turn in the big road. Then the WPA come in, and I was working on that road. Ned was in the way of the road, so we dug him up and made a good little box for his bones. He only had three teeth and one of them popped out when we dug him up. We put Ned in the box and moved him up to a good place on the hill, out of the way of the new road coming through. I can still take you to the exact spot where Nigger Ned is layin'.

"The Browns never had slaves. That was a hateful thing to own a nigger just like he was livestock. We are all Republicans ever since that slavery."

Henry was not through presenting the virtues of the Browns.

"Browns is all good people. We used to have good church meetin's in here. Ain't had any for quite some spell. There ain't no church in here. You can walk it out to Salt Gum or Dewitt, the closest churches we got, but there ain't many that ever does. And nowadays everyday is payday in a church. They dun you every time you go."

Henry's "eighth woman" is a small, dark-haired mountain woman who bustles about quietly, letting Henry speak for the family. But she listens, as she gathers scraps of wood in the yard for her cookstove or sits on the porch stringing green beans or sweeps at the porch and bare yard with a battered broom. But she agrees with most of what Henry says. She is a good woman for a Brown to have.

"That's right, I'm his eighth woman," she said. "I went by the name of Carrie Sizemore before me and Henry married." Henry and Carrie have six children: Wanda Lee, twenty; Roxie, eighteen; Glenn, sixteen; Quillie, fourteen; John Henry, twelve; and Stoney, seven.

"These young uns you see here are mine," Carrie Brown said. "Henry's other ones are all over. Lord, I can't count all his children. He had a regular swarm by one of his women."

And she added primly, "I suppose I'm about forty-seven, and I just been married twice."

Carrie Brown said Wanda Lee had been married "three years and over. But a woman couldn't get along with that man. She's back here now. Nobody can turn their own young uns off, can they?"

Henry says he thinks Wanda Lee and her husband will get back together. He plans to "drap down and see Judge Stivers about it." Judge Stivers was the man who spoke at the dedication of the new courthouse. Henry said the judge is a firm man on the bench.

"Brother, he runs that court. You can't hire a lawyer to speak up to him. A man comes in five minutes late, and Judge Stivers fines him $15. He come in five minutes late hisself once and fined himself right there—quick as a whip."

But where Henry is optimistic that Wanda Lee can repair her broken marriage, his woman is not so sure. She said with a quiet finality:

"Wanda Lee was asking for trouble. She married outside the family."

The marriage of Floyd and Rosie Brown lasted more than forty years despite their diverse personalities. Now, side by side in tiny houses, their relationship is more civil. Much more so, the Browns say, than during the marriage.

Rosie is large and strong, honest, outspoken, and thrifty. She has blue-gray eyes that peer frankly into yours. A graceful, lithe woman despite her age, she moves surely on large bare feet. Rosie is the intuitive mountain

Dewey Brown, Jr.

Burl Brown

housewife, following the habits of a lifetime, even though husband and children are now gone. Sweeping, washing. A big garden, pigs, the best boar in Browns Hollow; canning and preserving, always with a well-kept garden in summer and a reassuring woodpile in winter. Sensible and dependable.

Floyd is alternately despondent and carefree. Lounging in the hot summer sun, joking and smiling broadly. Or brooding. Then excitedly talking of someday walking out of Browns Hollow and seeing the world he has never seen. Floyd the dreamer, happy, likable, friendly, frivolous.

A hint of a breeze drifted down from Browns Hollow, and Rosie settled herself on a cane-bottomed chair on her porch to enjoy it. She tossed her reddish-crowned head toward the house next door. Floyd was not in evidence.

"He's my next-door neighbor now," Rosie said. She smiled a tolerant smile. "When he's in a good humor he's all right."

Rosie does not appear surprised that she did not hit it off with a Brown. "I'm a Taylor from Harlan County. I married Phillip Slusher first. He got killed in a mine in Virginia. I didn't have no children by him."

But she had the two boys and five girls by Floyd. One of them, Fred, dropped by to visit. Fred, in his forties, is devoted to both Rosie and Floyd and he drops by almost daily to talk and be sure illness has not struck either.

Fred may be the "typical" mountain man. Cautious and silent at first encounter; open and friendly when it is proved that the intruder has no interest in cutting welfare payments, is not looking for illegal whiskey, or just plain snooping. Lean and lithe, Fred Brown is a hard worker when there is work to do. But there rarely is much to do. He wears an ancient felt hat, its brim snapped up. His face is unshaven, and he has clear blue eyes like those of Rosie. Fred combines the characteristics of both his parents. Serious or joking, he quickly adapts to the mood of the conversation. Fred, like all the Browns, has his troubles, and like all mountaineers he keeps them in the family. When things bother him he goes to Rosie. He would never consider taking his troubles to an outsider.

Fred sat on the edge of the porch, squinting into the haze of the nearby mountain. "Knox is the hatefulest county there ever was," he said. "If it gets a chance to get a factory, they vote against it. Looks like they'd want jobs. I could use some work. I always worked. I hoed corn for fifty cents a day, ten hours a day for old man Bingham. He was a good man but he's gone. These days you go and get a sack of meal and it's a dollar and a half."

Rosie agreed: "You take a turn of corn in to get ground, and they'll take a gallon of it. It don't hardly pay to take in a turn of corn no more."

Fred shifted and scuffed his high-top shoes in the dust by the porch. Talk of hardship depresses him, and often, when poverty is being discussed, he will stubbornly try to change the subject.

"I was in the army," Fred said. "Austria, strangest kind of country. They had the blackest kind of light bread there ever was. And they didn't have much else to eat, from what I saw. I was plannin' to get married there in that Austria. But I give it up, and for a long time I'd get some letters from that girl.

"Had some good times. I had a friend in the army—big fleshy fellow. I was bad to drink, and he told them, 'You don't want no harm to come to this mountain boy.' He'd throw me in a truck and take me to the barracks, and I'd wake up in bed with no harm at all."

Somehow the talk always wandered back to current economics. Fred held out both hands, palms up, and gestured in exasperation.

"I tried to get on this project work. I traveled all the way to Barbourville, and that woman sat there, brother, with that blank, and put down that I had made some money. I told her the best truth I could. I figure that's what a man ought to do. I told her I sold a load of timbers. They had been timbered for some time, but I just sold them the day before for $28 and had to split with L. C. So my brother got $14 and I got $14, and that woman wrote it down and it knocked me clean out of the project work for a least a month."

Fred snorted a quick laugh of contempt for the workings of the bureaucratic mind, his eyes wide with wonder at the stupidity of welfare people who fill out blanks. Fred, mock humility in his voice, imitated the way he had pleaded his case to the woman.

"I said, 'Lady, how long you think a man can live on $14?'"

Then, as Rosie nodded agreement, Fred said in absolute disbelief, "She didn't put down ary thing to help me get on the project work."

The "project work" is one of the many facets of the welfare program extended to the mountains. It began about a year earlier as a pilot program financed by a federal grant. Its stated purpose was to provide aid for unemployed fathers. Now it has spread, and hundreds of mountain men are on it. They get $1.25 an hour for their work, and they are assigned to crews that clean up the creeks, cut weeds from the roads, and perform any other chores their assigned supervisors—county or city officials, school boards, magistrates—dream up.

In the towns, the crews are called "muskrat gangs" or "happy pappies." And businessmen tell many stories, accompanied by loud laughter, of muskrat gangs that plan to "strike" for better tools, longer lunch hours, or some such fringe benefit.

Where Rosie Brown is content to sit and let Fate dictate her life, Floyd is not. A restive spirit drives him still, as it has for all the sixty-eight years of his life. He had not been idle these past few years. He had many dreams, and one he was bound and determined to make come true. From his front porch he could see far up the green-draped walls of Johns Hollow, across the Middle Fork from Browns Branch. Since early spring, Floyd had been making daily trips up the hollow, trudging slowly, carrying lengths of rough, unplaned lumber.

Floyd planned to build a new house up that pretty hollow and see what adventures might await a man in a different place—a different hollow, but only a short walk from the one where he and Rosie raised their family. Not that he felt uncomfortable so close to his former wife. Floyd, in his way, still has a strong fondness for Rosie. Rosie's personal feelings are carefully shielded behind her fixed smile and unhinting blue-gray eyes, but Floyd's face changes with his emotions. Floyd is gregarious. He likes company. He appreciates a joke, and is rarely alone when he can find company. But when he speaks of Rosie his expression is wistful, like that of one of the eager. dogs that watch and wait expectantly, hoping, waiting for a scrap of food or a kind word.

At length, when Floyd did speak of Rosie, it was in a quiet tone and with a fleeting smile, more of remembrance than of humor. At that moment Floyd, the friendly Brown, was a solemn man—a man aging slowly and surely, just as the shack he lived in was aging. Aging and sagging and trying vainly to present an impression that nothing will ever change, fade, or pass away. A small man in Big Ben overalls, a khaki shirt, a brown hat and brown high-top shoes, he let his thoughts leap the ten feet to the cabin next door.

"Rose was my woman," Floyd said. "We lived together forty-five years, but we just couldn't do a gee-haw. We even got a divorce, a real legal one." He pushed gently at a huge fly crawling along his forearm, as though afraid he couldn't chase it away without harming it.

"We had good young uns, but to tell you the truth I don't call all their ages. I could study on it awhile and come pretty dern close. I know our youngest, Geneva, married Garrett Brown. He's some relation, but not much."

The recollections had a hypnotic effect on Floyd. His eyes narrowed, and he leaned back against the weathered wood of his cabin wall. His voice grew even softer while he was looking at some private picture his memory super-imposed upon the mountain across the hollow.

"I got two wives dead and one ain't. But now she ain't my wife. I don't slight her. I do pretty well by her. I don't have nothing she can't have. And the young uns . . . I treat them all just as well as I do ary soul. I ain't got no little ones left at home. I got forty-two grandchildren.

"It was good to raise them here. I been here a good sight of years. I can remember old man Steve Brown. He was the first one in. I seen him once. He musta been a hundred and ten years old. I was just a little boy. Old Man Steve was a big tall-looking fellow. He farmed and used to be a pretty good liver. He had plenty to live on. Used to have the awfullest lot of cattle. I seen over a hundred head of turkeys oncet that was his'n."

Floyd fell silent for long moments, still looking quietly at something in the distance that recalled the years gone by in Browns Hollow. When he spoke again it was without a hint of malice or blame.

"I'll tell you what hurts a lot of fellows when they get old. It's women cussin' and villifyin'. You live together and raise a good family. Seven. That's a good family. Times was hard. I worked many a day for a quarter, and thought I was doing well. I could buy meat for a nickel a pound."

A few days later Floyd was through carrying rough lumber and nails and tools up the inviting trail that followed Johns Branch. Early in the morning his son, Fred, joined him, and they began to build Floyd's dream house.

There was a dirt logging road that followed the base of the mountain and at one place it widened. Here was the spot Floyd had picked. The cabin would be far enough off the road to prevent a careless logging truck from knocking it onto the valley floor below.

Floyd and Fred piled rocks to support the four corners of the cabin, level-ing them by carefully squatting and sighting so the floor of the cabin would be true. When the corners were fixed for a cabin eleven by fourteen feet, the floor was placed on. Joists first, then rough planking for the floor.

Hammering steadily and rhythmically, the two men worked throughout the day. They worked in the steady, productive manner of the mountain carpenter—pick up a board, sight critically along its edge, then put it in place. Not a board was rejected. The strokes of the hammers echoed along Johns Hollow. Three blows—occasionally four—to embed a size-sixteen nail in the seasoned second-grade wood.

By midafternoon of the second day the building was completed. Father and son stood in the middle of the road to admire their handiwork. Smiling and sweating from the exertion, they stood and looked. It was a good job, and their smiles showed their approval.

Floyd Brown and his new house on Johns Branch

"They hardly wouldn't let nothing like this sit in a town," Fred said.

His father cackled in appreciation, and the two went inside to escape the blazing sun. Before dark, Floyd had moved in.

A door and a window faced the road. The other walls were solid wood. "It's good," Floyd said. "All a man needs is a stay place, and I'll take this as good as any."

For Floyd, who lives on social security, the new house represents a staggering investment. Besides the nails, he had bought four rolls of roofing paper and a window from a lumber company for $19. "Graded-out" lumber costs around $35 a thousand board feet, and Floyd figures, "I've got more than $70 just in the lumber."

But it was well worth the sacrifice. When Floyd and his son sat in the new house on that first day, Floyd was a happy man as he let his gaze wander slowly and proudly around his new surroundings. Just inside the door a wooden shelf supported a galvanized bucket of water, a metal dipper, and a washbasin. A face towel hung from a nail above the shelf. There was a black round wood-burning cookstove, its flue sprouting up through a hole in the roof. Behind the stove, a large skillet, a small skillet, and a square black bread pan hung from their carefully spaced nails.

Along the rear wall was a large kitchen table, its uneven legs resting on wood chips. On the table were placed a length of worn oilcloth, a huge box of Country Gentlemen chewing tobacco, a box of crackers, and a carton of nonfat dry milk with the familiar stenciled notation "U.S. Department of Agriculture."

In the corner diagonally across from the door, four large nails supported Floyd's spare clothing: a pair of pants, a few shirts, a heavy coat, a sweater and his hat, now that he was relaxing at home.

Along the end wall opposite the shelf and stove, Floyd placed his iron folding bed with its two quilts and one wool blanket. It was unmade with a look of permanence. There were two oft-repaired chairs for eating and for guests. Floyd was sure there would be guests from time to time. Floyd and Fred lay back on the disheveled bed, one across either end, and studied the interior furnishings with approval.

When the inspection was complete—from door to shelf to stove to table to bed, the attention of the two men came naturally to the window in the front wall of the house. Its millwork was meticulous, and the panes of glass were unbroken and crystal clear. Its installation, however, was something short of professional standards. The two men studied the rough pieces that held the window in place in silence.

Floyd spoke first: "I 'spect we did a rough job on that window."

Floyd was too happy in his new surroundings to let a piece of rough carpentry dim his enthusiasm. He pursed his lips thoughtfully, crinkled the corners of his eyes, and rationalized: "Well, sir, if a man'd pass here on a gallopin' horse, he wouldn't hardly notice that window no way."

It was a time to talk and visit and relax and enjoy. Moving into the new house was a milestone in Floyd's life, the first since the day years ago when he had moved out of Rosie's life and next door. Floyd and Fred, father and son, talked earnestly, in the way of mountain men, of things they knew and remembered, the scope of their conversation bounded by the confines of their experiences and interests in the narrow steep depression that is Browns Hollow.

"Times seems better already," Floyd said. "I used to haul a sled of coal —about half a ton at a time—over that mountain, me and mule together, for one dollar. Had to make it snappy to get in two loads in a day. Now you couldn't get a mess of meat for one eatin' for a quarter."

Fred nodded agreement. "They used to be people had ten or fifteen head of cattle and pigs in here," he said. "You want a pig, you just go out and catch you one. I used to be out tater planting, and there'd be one or two big sows with a litter of pigs on them. Nobody ever come after them. Folks had so many hogs they jest didn't care. Hogs'd come in here from Clay County. Now people are worser over a little pig than they were over a good milk cow then."

"They was plenty of everything," Floyd said. "I seen pie plants—some calls them rhubub—big as your arm."

Talk of pie plants reminded Floyd of the one thing in life he doesn't like —cooking for himself. He arose and started to poke and putter around the stove.

"I sure get tired of can biscuits," he said.

He took the eight-by-ten-inch black bread pan from its nail and tilted a wooden box against the rear of the stove. "I'll show you something real handy," he volunteered. He set the pan on the upturned, tilted end of the box inches from the rear of the round stove.

"Cook biscuits there," he said. "They get the right heat and they bake by the time you can fry meat."

Floyd kept his eyes on the black bread pan, and muttered: "I'm going to try myself the hardest I can to get a woman. A man gets tired of cooking."

"Oh, yes you will," Fred said mockingly.

Floyd grinned. "You need a woman," he said. "Why, I've got pieces of beef in the store froze so hard you can't cut it with a knife. Can't even beat it with a hammer. By the time it's a day or two old and gets thawed out, the taste's all gone out of it." He hefted the pan, then placed it back on the nail. "You can't beat women for cooking."

"Lissen," Fred said in disbelief.

"You watch," Floyd said, winking at his son. "I got plenty lumber for another room. I'm going to get me a long-haired woman. It's been fifteen years, and a man can't go much longer than that."

Fred laughed at the old man's enthusiasm.

"What do you know?" Floyd demanded, his eyes glittering with his relish of the idea. "I might be in Cuby this time next week."

Fred shook his head, casting a negative shroud over the whole idea.

Floyd was undismayed. " 'Cause I ain't gone there yet is no cause to keep me from taking a notion to."

When dusk approaches on Stinking Creek, the sun glides slowly toward the mountaintops in the west. Then it lingers and floats as though reluctant to end its day's journey across the blue sky. At the final moment, however, it gathers speed and plunges quickly behind a mountain, immediately casting a purple twilight haze over the hollow. The sun was lingering, as though waiting for a celestial signal to dip behind the mountain, when Fred took his leave. Outside, he paused and took a final approving look at the house; then he was gone.

It was time for Floyd's first meal in his new home, and he said he'd like to make it "a fiittin' one." But first, he must go down to Hubbard's store. He latched the front door from the inside and crawled out the single window. Once outside, he jerked out the supporting stick that held the window up and let it crash to the sill, thus shutting the house.

At the store he stared at the shelves and debated the ingredients of his first feast in his new house. At length he decided: a can of Kewpie Whole Kernel Golden Corn, a can of Red Gold Tomato Juice, and a dozen eggs. It came to a dollar.

"Put it on the credit," Floyd told the youth behind the counter.

Floyd shrugged off an offer of a ride back to the house. It was a time to be alone, a turning point, a new beginning, and Floyd will sit and cook and eat and sleep in his new house perhaps for years—until his restive spirit drives him on. Up another hollow, perhaps, but probably never to "Cuby."

All the Browns know about Floyd's new house—knew about it from the moment it was finished, although there was never an outward sign of it being discussed. When asked, "Did you know Floyd has a new house?" the answer would be, "I heered it." But no discussion. Floyd's new house is Floyd's

Charley **Brown**

business, and not a fit subject for a Brown to be kicking around in loose conversation. Even Henry the spokesman said, "I heered it, brother."

But the code that forbids unseeming talk of the whys and hows of Floyd's house also demands an attempt at decent conversation when one who is friendly to Browns Hollow wants to talk. So there was always a willingness to talk, to smile, to shake hands: the men with big rough hands outstretched; the women with quick tentative smiles cast quickly from the gloom inside the doorways; the children, wide-eyed and watching, their eyes begging for approval—like surprised angels that only recently had unexpectedly tumbled somehow into the dust.

What to talk about? The same principles that apply anywhere in the world apply in Browns Hollow. You talk about what comes to mind.

In the bars at Hazard, Kentucky, where alcohol is legal, you talk with the traveling salesmen who "make" that part of the state. The subjects that come to mind: "The sales manager is a bastard. I can do more with this territory than any man they ever put in here. I can milk an expense account as well as the next man."

In the courthouses you discuss the declining fortunes of the Republican Party, the stupidity of the state rulers in Frankfort, the absolute unreliability of the press.

In Browns Hollow, you discuss what comes to mind. You sit on the porch or gather on the lone couch and big double bed of the "front room," and talk —but slowly, taking turns, almost as though every speaker had his alloted number of minutes, and no more. You talk while children swarm in and out, as though constantly searching. A little girl shyly edging across the floor to the point where she can run for the door. A toddler clutching a soggy biscuit. A mother nursing a baby. The baby is put on the floor, but the big breast remains bare. An unnerving sight, like the big brown eye of a melancholy calf watching your every move.

Or you stand out in the yard, ignoring the dust, and discuss what comes to mind. Charley Brown finds social security comes to mind. The big man who took charge masterfully at the breeding of Cordie's sow has his moments of worry. He needs the social security.

"I can't read, but I got my birth certificate. It cost $8, and then they wouldn't talk about it to give me the social security."

Charley sighed and kicked a round loose stone into the creek at his doorstep. "Back in Roosevelt's day I worked on this road right here with the WPA."

He hasn't done much since, but he lives. "They give me $138 a month welfare for the children." He has a large family. "Well, I got—I reckon—

let's see." Charley's brow crinkled with the mental effort. "I got Loretto there, that's one; Pauline, that's two. . . ." The lips kept moving, but the remainder of the calculation was performed in silence. Then Charley announced, "I got five girls and four boys living and four boys dead and one girl."

To raise this family, he gets the $138 and surplus commodities. But he has had some bad luck. None recently, but enough to make a man cautious and content to leave well enough alone. "I mind my business. I don't want no part of a town or a jailhouse."

And who knows when disaster might strike?

"I cut my finger oncet and it sot up blood pizen. I never crooked it in six months. Nearly kilt me."

If there is anything Charley is proud of, it is his father. Mountain fathers have a way of leaving an aura of greatness for their children to discuss and rehash over the years, long after the old man is laid to rest high on the hillside, a pine or oak tree nearby to shade him while he waits for the Resurrection.

"My dad cotched four hundred children," Charley said with a welling of pride. "He was a midwife doctor. He went out on nights wasn't fit for stock to be out to cotch a baby. He was the best midwife doctor in the state of Kentucky."

And there is friendly conversation down the creek at the home of Bowman Brown. If not conversation, a smile of welcome from Lilly Mae, who is fourteen and has never gone to school. Lilly Mae, quiet, uncommunicative, bare feet protruding from her long dress, sitting on a stump or rock, listening, smiling at the conversation, rarely joining it.

And quick, eager talk from twelve-year-old Betsy, a pretty dark-haired, alert child who takes care of her younger brothers and sisters. She holds eight-month-old L. B. on her slender hip and watches three-year-old David with one eye as she talks, a flash of white teeth in her smile. Betsy, at twelve, the little housekeeper, watching the little ones while her parents are busy elsewhere, even cooking for them.

Once, while she was slicing meat, the heavy butcher knife slipped and opened a deep gash along her thumb. Betsy was alone with the small ones. Holding the bleeding hand out and away from her, she mixed flour and coal oil with the other, applied the resulting pasty mixture to the wound, bound it in a bit of dirty cloth, and resumed preparing supper. Later, Betsy laughed about it. "Like to bled me to death," she said.

Dewey Brown is Henry's brother. They call Dewey "Preacher." But he doesn't preach much anymore. Nobody preaches or prays much anymore in Browns Hollow. What does Dewey think of as he sits before his crowded little house? Of his grandfather who came first to the valley. Of the good times that were, and the bad times that are.

"Hit was just a walking path when he come by here—old man Steve Brown. He just walked in carrying his grubbing hoe and his shooting rifle. There was some real timber here then. And game. Millions of dollars' worth of timber been cut off and burned. There ain't no game. The govermint tried to turn deer loose in here, and the fox hunters run them off."

And there is Dewey's wife: small, dark-haired, tired but friendly. She invites you to take the huge, almost impossible step up from the ground and into the cabin. There are no steps. She knows about Floyd's new house, but pretends you didn't mention it.

"Rosie, that's my mother. Floyd's not my father, though. L. C. and Fred is my brothers, but I ain't seen Fred in several months."

The children mill in and out of the room. There are an upright cedar chest, a brown sofa, a cot covered with a red blanket, an iron double bed. And a TV set. "We can't get nothin' but Channel Six." There is another room that has two double beds, and a kitchen that extends across the back of both the rooms.

Her family is healthy. "I got nine here, one married, but they broke up. I got five girls and five boys. We draw social security and welfare for the youngsters. Just enough to get by on—about $60 welfare and about $60 social security. We get the commodities, too."

Mrs. Dewey Brown, in a shapeless rust-colored dress, holds and nurses a baby in a diaper made from bright blue material. She proudly smiles at her children. "They all like beans, taters, cabbage, and chicken. Every last one eats pretty hearty. We got a little bottom of corn planted. Dewey there is sixty-four, and not able to work much."

Four-year-old Judy Ann, blond and wide-eyed with the haunting beauty of mountain children, tugged at her mother, until she gave her a safety pin from a row fastened to the front of her dress. Little Judy Ann stuck it happily in the front of her own dress, and then wheedled another. One by one. Each time, coming back to her mother, she said, "Gimme 'nother pretty."

One advantage of living in Browns Hollow: nobody, even a welfare worker, hardly ever passes that way.

"Oh, the county did come and rake a little dirt over the rocks in the road, and then it washed right off. Hobert Mills was only one ever did nothin' when he was a squire. He brought in a bulldozer and they shot some of the rocks out. Before that, they just come in and made mudholes for the kids to go to school in."

Mrs. Dewey Brown moved to the doorway and prepared her beans for supper. She broke off the ends of the long pale-green pods, and pulled off the strings, which were tossed into the yard, where the chickens fought for them. Then she broke the beans and piled them in the pot. She got water from a well consisting of an open pipe reaching down into the rocky earth; above it was a frame of saplings and a pully through which passed a rope knotted from many pieces. The water had a smell, but it gradually disappeared—almost—as the beans bubbled hour after hour together with a piece of salted white side meat.

A few yards up the road, Henry sat on his porch with the commanding view, and waited. He assumes that a visitor to Browns Hollow will pay his respects there before leaving. It is not wise to ignore Henry. He sat rubbing the blond head of Stoney, his youngest. "Stoney is my baby," Henry said. "There might not be no more out of me." His face relaxed into a look of unmasked devotion as he watched Stoney vainly try to avoid his father's hands.

When the boy finally fled, Henry turned and said: "Me and Fred got a hoss trade to make. You welcome to come along, honey."

Honey.

Don't smile. "Honey" is a word of friendship, like the western cowboy's "podner" or the soldier's "buddy." Big, powerful men, men who haul down logs and can fell a mule with a fist, use the word. Not an effeminate word, it is a term whose origin nobody seems to know. As visit after visit goes by, the word is used more and more.

"Come to the hoss trade if you care to, honey."

Henry, as did every man in Browns Hollow, wanted Fred's horse. It is a beautiful animal, spotted, muscled, graceful, and strong. It can outrun anything in Browns Hollow—outwork anything, too.

Henry brought his black pony and met Fred down near where Browns Branch empties into Middle Fork of Stinking Creek. The spot is on the creek bank directly behind the house Floyd recently deserted for his dream house on Johns Branch. The preliminaries to the horse trade had begun days before. Whenever the two men had met, they had discussed trading the black pony for the horse. But because this was the day of the formal trading, there was an air of seriousness as the little party gathered on the creek bank. The principals: Henry, his thumbs hooked in his overall bib; Fred, unsmiling and respectfully waiting for the older man to speak first; Glenn, Henry's boy, holding the reins of the pony; Alvin, Fred's boy, leading the spotted horse. The two boys led the horse and the pony to one side, and waited silently.

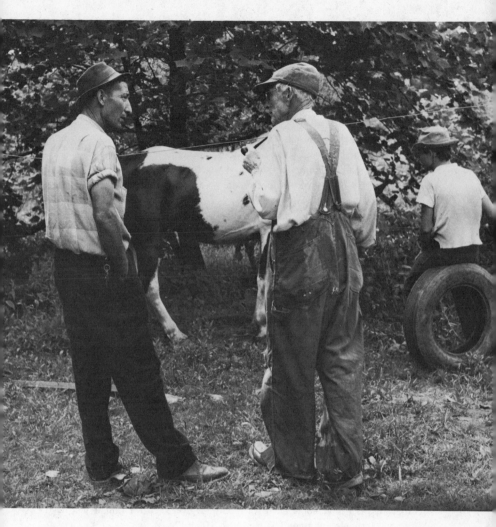

The hoss trade: Fred Brown, left, and Henry. Henry's boy Glenn is sitting on an old tire at right.

Henry and Fred walked a few yards away, like two combatants nearing the time of their trial. The bystanders remained at a discreet distance, a few of the Brown men and boys quietly giving the two men room to talk and trade. The two men ignored the pony and the horse.

Henry began the trade: "I'm satisfied that's the best hoss in Kentucky, Fred."

Fred scratched himself. "That hoss is eight year old, and you can hold him with one hand and whup him with the other."

Henry made a humming sound of assent. He was not going to argue the obvious merits of the horse, an animal admired by all of Browns Hollow.

"I reckon he's strong as pig iron," Henry said.

"You jest can't balk him," Fred said. "You tie him to that house, and he'll pull 'til he falls out.. He's strong, and he never had a bite of corn. And he won't kick you."

Henry sought a standoff in this characteristic. "That pony won't kick you, either. You can't make him kick you."

Fred listened politely to the older man's extolling of the pony's gentle temperment. But the tone of his voice indicated he had dismissed the point as debatable. "I been logging with that hoss, and fall and catch on to his tail and he still wouldn't kick me."

Henry abandoned the discussion of the relative reluctance to kick of the two animals. He walked away a few steps, peered into the creek as though fascinated by something he saw there, then turned back to Fred:

"I'll give you that pony and a brand-new collar I bought for him for a $5 bill and $40 to boot." His voice was lower and more earnest. He made no attempt to conceal his desire for the strong spotted hoss. I'm going to sell that mule of mine, Fred, and if I don't sell right away, I'll go to the bank and get it."

A look of sadness spread across Fred's face. "The only reason I'm trading that hoss is I have some need for money. I give $170 for him. I just need it now. I know you're good as the bank, Henry."

"Forty-five dollars," Henry said.

The expression on Fred's face deepened into melancholy. "I told you $50. You come to me and ask me the lowest I'd swap for, and that's what I told you."

Henry gripped the frayed bib of his overalls until white appeared among the purple and brown on his hands, hands that ached for the big, powerful hoss. "I'll just pay you the $50 of money and keep the collar," he said. He moved a step nearer the two animals, but still not looking at them. Fred's voice, sad but firm as the rocky ground on which he stood, brought Henry up short. "You said t'other night I'd get the collar."

The old man turned and managed a look of amazement on his weathered face. "Fifty dollars in greenbacks. You can't kick out now, Fred."

But Fred was again in the throes of melancholy. His face grieved for the lost trade, as though with urging, tears would flow down the stubble on his face. "You know'd my price, Henry. You know'd it good as you please. Fifty dollars and the collar along with the black pony."

Henry snorted gently. The snort signaled the end of negotiations. Henry turned and walked toward an outhouse that leaned against the creek bank. As he disappeared inside, Fred turned to his boy Alvin. "Take the hoss back home and turn him out." Fred said. The two boys led the two animals away, and Fred climbed up and out of the low place beside the creek. When Henry emerged from the outhouse, he was alone. When he saw that Fred and the boys were gone, he let a smile come to his face and said, with open admiration: "Fred's a good hoss trader. But I ain't through with him yet, honey."

On a hot afternoon in late summer, Floyd found the joy of his new home waning, and his gregarious nature drove him down from the hollow to the place where the creeks fork. Henry was there, sitting in the shade on the porch of Floyd's old, now abandoned, house. And one by one various men of the Brown clan came by to talk. The topic of interest in Browns Hollow was still Henry's attempts to trade Fred out of his horse.

Next door, Rosie came out and settled into a cane-bottomed chair to rest on her porch. Her presence influenced the conversation. All the men— except Floyd—turned to glance toward Rosie. Rosie ignored them.

Henry was sitting on the edge of the porch, his high-topped shoes resting on the dust. He studied the sad look on Floyd's face, and tried to cheer him. "Women is strange," he said.

Floyd's eyes quickly came around to study the old man's profile. But Henry was looking at the dust beneath him. His voice was both mocking and serious: "With women you got to have something to bait them. You know what I'd do if I had that little house of Floyd's up on the hill? I'd bring me a woman in there some night and have me somebody to sleep with. I bet within thirty days Floyd'll have a woman in there."

Floyd's eyes crinkled with gratitude for the light turn of the conversation. His mood switched abruptly, the way a quiet pool in the creek changes when a large stone is hurled into it. He chuckled.

"Only way I got to get one in that hollow is pack her in," he said. "I can't drive no car." He pursed his lips as though in deep thought. "An' I don't know . . . I been burnt so bad." Then a wide grin. "Sometimes I get so hot I figure and figure on it."

Henry was like an adult soothing a child now. "Why, Floyd, you're about as well off without a woman. My young uns takes care of me better than most women."

For the first time, Floyd let his glance wander to Rosie's front porch. Rosie sat there out of earshot, calm, serene.

Henry saw the glance. To no one in particular, he observed: "Some men just let a woman run away with them. Some men go wild-crazy with them. If you keep your mind on a woman, you're gone."

As he talked, a new member joined the group. Weaving unsteadily on rubbery legs, a big blond man lurched over and leaned against a porch post. A medicine bottle jutted from the sagging side pocket of his trousers. His watery blue eyes were filmed over, and he smelled of the putrid, stinging aroma of moonshine that has encountered an unstable stomach. As Henry spoke, the man nodded in sanctimonious agreement. Then he stepped around the corner of the ancient shack and took a long drink of the colorless fluid in the medicine bottle. When he came back, Henry was sitting silently. Floyd arose, brushed himself off with the palms of his hands, and walked toward Rosie's house—the house that was once his and Rosie's.

Henry still stared at the dust, but the big blond man watched Floyd's progress sadly. Moisture gathered in his eyes. To Floyd's departing back, he said, almost sobbing: "Where your heart is, your treasure is. That's in the Bible."

"Your woman, that's your whole life," Henry agreed.

The man with the bottle held to the porch post for support. His shirt was wet with sweat, and his left hand reached as though of its own will for the medicine bottle in his pocket. He squinted through the bright sunshine until his bloodshot eyes finally came into focus on Floyd, now standing in front of Rosie's porch, talking with his former wife. The big man's hand pulled the bottle free of his pocket, and his voice was thick with emotion:

"He thirsts after her and she thirsts after him, and now he's done moved in that little house up Johns Hollow."

6 Shall We Gather at the River...

ACROSS THE MOUNTAIN from Browns Hollow the same sun beat down mercilessly and the same dust draped the trees beside the rocky roads in powdery shrouds. But here in the larger hollow, along the mainstream of Stinking Creek, a breath of hope was stirring.

Preacher Marsee was prevailed upon by the congregation of Salem Baptist Church to conduct a week-long revival. "I hope to do the best I can with the strength the Lord gives me," he said solemnly when the plans were announced. At Messer's store, at the stony, drying junctions of the creeks, wherever men met there was talk of Preacher Marsee's revival—the first in a long time for Stinking Creek.

Preacher Marsee was worried. Converts had been few at the regular every-other-Sunday services, and a revival without converts could be a disservice to the Lord of unspeakable proportions. In the small concrete block post office and grocery at Mills, they asked with open concern, "Reckon how many the preacher will get to come forward?"

But nobody would venture a guess. Most good church members vowed to attend the nightly preachin's and lend what moral support they could.

The revival began on a hot, still Monday night as the heat waves shimmered from the church roof and its tiny bell-less steeple. Long before the sun fell beyond the mountain, the young people gathered at the church. For an hour or more they stood or sat on the shady side, talking quietly. They watched the old people arrive as the hour of the revival grew near, and when Preacher Marsee at length stood at the pulpit in shirt sleeves, the little church was crowded.

It did not take long to see that the revival was to be successful. On the third night, eight people came forward at the end of the service to shake Preacher Marsee's outstretched hand and to be enlisted in the fold of the church. Preacher Marsee, elated and flushed with the exertion, stepped up the tempo of the revival.

For a week he extolled the virtues of heaven, the forgiveness of sin. His slightly nasal, sincere voice echoed around the little church; his exhortations were like an enveloping arm, guiding, urging, pleading with the people of Stinking Creek to prepare themselves for the day of the Resurrection.

Long before the regular morning services on the following Sunday, it was evident that the revival would be extended. So for two weeks the church echoed with the shouts and pleadings of Preacher Marsee as twilight came to the creek each evening, and the strong voices of the singers could be heard far beyond Buckeye Fork. It was assured that the revival would leave additional spotless souls in Stinking Creek and that the rolls of the church would grow.

On the first Sunday after the revival began, an elderly lady stood in front of the church before the morning service.

"'Peers you'll have to wait a spell to see our baptizing," she said, almost gleefully. "There'll be a heap more to jine yit," she predicted. "No tellin' when Preacher will wind up."

He wound up after two weeks, and the baptizing of the converts from the revival was set for the second Sunday. What few problems arose were minor. The creek, running raw with acid from the old coal mine, caused concern among some, and the leaders of the church discussed the possibility of "digging a little baptizing hole" in the small trickle that was Buckeye Fork. This idea was abandoned.

The traditional baptizing place for both the Baptists and the members of the Holiness Church, which sits farther up the hollow, is a deep hole in the bed of Stinking Creek directly in front of Gilbert Bargo's house. Consequently, Bargo has seen many a baptizing. He walks down to the creek to participate in those of his own church, but when the members of the Holiness Church arrive for a baptizing, Bargo merely watches from his field, impressed.

"They sure have some jubilee," he said.

Although the creek was shrunken from the dry spell, the hole at Bargo's house was about the best place along its course. But an objection was raised. Someone saw a dead cat in the creek there, and reported it to the congregation. A fear of the acid and reddish iron precipitate in the creek, coupled with this new information, caused abandonment of the spot.

The place finally chosen was a mile or so upstream near Shady School where Trace Branch trickles into Stinking Creek. The hole there was shallow; but fortunately a rain began a few days before the ceremony, and the creek, although turbid with clay and silt, was deep enough for baptizing. The increased flow that resulted from the rains swept down the narrow creek bed and temporarily flushed out or covered the unsightly cans, bottles, and other trash that clings to the rocky banks when the creek is low.

On the day of the baptizing the creek bank was crowded with the congregation and bystanders. A swinging bridge which crosses at that point groaned on its supporting rusty steel cables as watchers gathered on it to seek a vantage point. It was a hot Sunday morning when even the big purple flies seemed loathe to expend sufficient energy to fly.

But the congregation was eager and happy, pushing to the very edge of the creek through the scrub sycamore and willow growth, ignoring the gray, sticky mud, and moving closer to the sanctified spot where sixteen souls were about to step nearer the Kingdom of Heaven.

The sixteen were all young people, gathered in a knot by the creek. Some of the girls wore tinted, transparent raincoats over their dresses, the coats tied tightly about them against the turbid yellow water of the creek. The older children were quiet and willing; the little ones gathered about Preacher Marsee, their eyes wide with apprehension as they wondered at the fervor of the singing that arose from the multitude gathered at the creek bank.

Suddenly, Preacher Marsee, in a white shirt open at the throat, led his converts into the creek. He was at the head of the long winding line, as those to be baptized followed one by one, each holding hands with both the person in front and the person in back. The young people entered the creek downstream from the crowd, then waded up to the spot where the water deepened to waist height on the smaller ones. Preacher Marsee led the new members of his flock, carefully feeling the way with his feet, smiling, his face turned upward into the scalding sun. Preacher Marsee was collecting the fruits of his two weeks of struggle with evil in the hot little box that was Salem Baptist Church in midsummer.

When he reached the baptizing hole, Preacher Marsee turned and brought the first child to his side. Placing a napkin over the little girl's face, Preacher Marsee said in a voice that was ecstatic to the point of almost sounding like a series of gasps:

"Upon this profession of faith in Christ as your Saviour and Lord, and in obedience to His command, I baptize you my sister, in the name of the Father and the Son and the Holy Ghost."

With that, he plunged the child beneath the murky water, lowering her backward so that the water closed over her face with a quick gush, then raised her quickly.

The
Baptizing

As the child went beneath the water, a chorus of voices shattered the quiet of the congregation as a hymn began:

>*"Shall we gather at the river,*
>*The beautiful, the beautiful river . . ."*

One by one the line edged nearer Preacher Marsee as he repeated the ritual: "Upon this profession of faith . . ."

A boy or a girl was plunged into the yellow stream. And the chorus resumed:

>*"Shall we gather at the river*
>*That flows by the throne of God."*

For Preacher Marsee it was a moment of triumph. In two short weeks his apprehensions as to the success of a revival had been swept away in a victory for his Maker. Now in the role of spokesman for a conqueror, he exulted. He clasped a boy to him, and before performing the ritual of baptism, turned to the crowd, and cried: "I feel so good. I could do this all day. Thank God! Whole families saved!"

And when the next convert stepped forward, Preacher Marsee cried, "The angels are hovering over this creek today, and the Lord is looking down."

As the believer was plunged into the water, the voices on the bank sang:

>*"Shall we gather at the river,*
>*The beautiful, the beautiful river . . ."*

And from those on the bridge, the hymn echoed along the narrow valley:

>*"Shall we gather at the river*
>*That flows by the throne of God."*

When the last of the sixteen young residents of Stinking Creek were baptized, they waded out of the creek and into the arms of their weeping parents. Some—the very young—trembled as though from a chill—but more from excitement—as their wet bodies were embraced by the emotional throng.

Preacher Marsee, the last to emerge from the creek, stepped out onto the bank elated and flushed with success. He held out his hand in greeting, but a quick sad look played upon his face, now wet with perspiration and red from the sun and heat.

"Thank you. Thank you," he cried to the searing blue sky. He paused a moment, and his voice was a whisper when he added, "We have only touched the hem of His garment today."

A few days later the runoff from the rains had passed by, and the creek was only inches deep. The air of sanctity was gone, and the green sycamore and willow thickets looked more like hopeless second growth than the bright green drapes they had appeared to be on the day of the baptizing. The dying creek could no longer conceal the pieces of broken glass, cans, old shoes, Purex bottles, and litter that lay along its bottom. The rounded stones, stained from their long contact with the polluted water, appeared to be more of a poisonous hue than the princely red tone they had assumed during the magic of the baptizing. The widening banks of the shrinking creek were now an expanse of gummy gray mud, occasionally marked by the tracks of some tiny creature which had passed that desolate way.

A man walked out on the swinging bridge and stared down. He was chewing on a long green blade of Johnson grass, and after a few minutes of silence he removed the blade and said, "I reckon we shouldn't oughta throw that stuff in the creek."

7 Shady School

THE CHILDREN OF Stinking Creek are beautiful—strikingly, physically beautiful. Their faces are open and frank, and they reflect the round, fair features of their English, Scottish, and Irish ancestors. Even when filthy and clothed in rags stiffened with accumulations of grease and grime, mountain children bring you up short with their wide trusting eyes and their angelic, innocent, naïve friendliness.

Despite shortages of food, proper medical attention, and lack of sanitation, the children of Stinking Creek appear to bloom with a sweetness that defies their heritage. But while their physical beauty is exceptional, their intellectual world is shabby.

In the county seat that serves Stinking Creek, a man who stood high in school administration once said,, "I don't know whether we can ever do anything for those people up the hollows."

Whether anything can or cannot be done, one thing is apparent: No one has ever tried to do anything.

The beautiful children who live on the long middle stretch of Stinking Creek first drink of the fountain of human knowledge at Shady School, as children have for years. It is a tasteless draft. Shady School is neither shady nor a school, except in name. A small one-room building, unkempt, with paint peeling from dirty outside walls, it has a rusted well with a squeaking pump for water; and the two inevitable rotting, stinking outhouses marked "Girls" and "Boys." When a child begins his intellectual growth at Shady School, he is taking his first definite step toward lifelong dependency.

Grubby Shady School sits full in the glare of the sun, and inside it is sickening hot in the warm months. To compensate for this, it is freezing in the winter months—except for the circle of intense warmth that encircles the potbellied stove in the center of the room like an invisible wall. There is no proper distance to sit from the stove. One is either too hot or too cold.

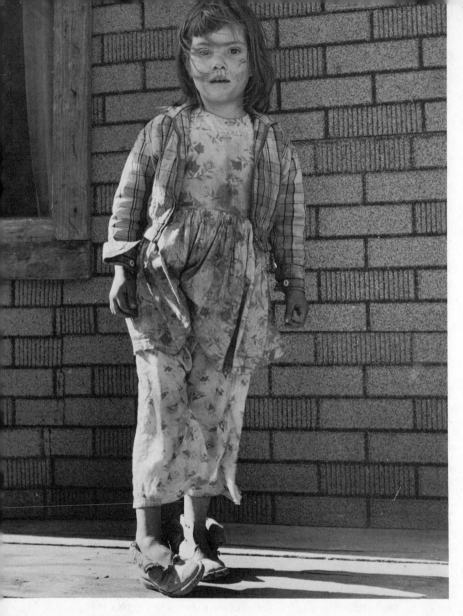

Peggy Sizemore

On a hot day in May the big windows were closed against any invasion by the occasional hot breeze. The door to the tiny porch was open, exhaling a rich aroma of urine and sweating children, the pungent smell of twenty-seven bodies that made up the first, second, and third grades. They ranged in age from a five-year-old girl to a fifteen-year-old boy.

At the center of the room, beside the rusty stove, two coal scuttles spilled their load of waste paper, milk cartons from the day before, and other debris onto the worn, unpainted four-inch seasoned boards of the floor. At the rear, a leaking water bucket dribbled its tepid contents onto a widening dark wet place on the floor. The table that held the water bucket and its dipper also holds various bits of clothing and an occasional stray book.

Across the front of the room, behind the raised platform that supports the teacher's desk, a double-section blackboard was filled with the spelling words of the day:

direction	aisles
blow	greatest
please	nation
pleasure	coast
least	sailors
seventeen	breakfast

The first-graders were nodding drowsily along the windows to the left as the children in the two upper grades read for the teacher, Mrs. Sue Zigos, who at the age of twenty-two was in her first year as a teacher. She was assigned to this desolate educational outpost by a school board which offers her little support. Mrs. Zigos doesn't like her job. She liked teaching, but not at Shady. She must drive the twenty miles from Barbourville each day, and Shady, she finds, is not an exciting place after her practice-teaching classes the year before in the modern school at the county seat.

"They don't have nothing here to work with," Mrs. Zigos said. She is a quiet, attractive girl with reddish-blond hair and blue eyes. She sat at her big desk up front on the raised platform and looked unhappily over her charges. But she strives for an appearance of enthusiasm. In her white blouse and brown plaid skirt with its thin straw belt and brown slippers, she looked very much the part of the college student she was only a year ago. She is from the mountains, and she was educated in the mountains at Union College in Barbourville. Her husband, Wayne, works in the post office at the college.

Mrs. Zigos was obviously trying. But twenty-seven children in three grades and on a dozen different achievement levels is a challenge that would cause some of the best teachers in the best of schools to hesitate. Twenty-seven

Mrs. Sue Zigos, teacher at Shady School

Shady School

children, many with illiterate parents; few with magazines or newspapers at home; many waiting for the day when they can quit the tedious trek to school in outlandish weather.

"We don't have much to do with," Mrs. Zigos said. Her transparent, fair complexion was pink from the heat. Perspiration on her forehead made tiny ringlets of the hair that touched her skin there. "They don't have paper half the time. In town they are quieter and more alert. Their families have more money. They come in contact with more. Well, it was just a lot easier."

Mrs. Zigos has a soft mountain accent, just as the children do. "I was raised over on Jeff Creek," she said. "I was a Bargo. My mother was a Mills, and my father died when I was nine years old. I drawed—drew—a war veteran's child's pension to go to school on."

She sighed, fanned herself, and smiled. "Shady. I don't know how they ever got that name. With three grades the problem is keeping the others working while I'm working with one group. Each grade should be divided into three levels, but we can't do it."

School at Shady is pretty much an open-house affair. You drop in when you like. You begin your education at your leisure and you end it with a whim. One thirteen-year-old girl had started when she was nine. Others bring their little brothers and sisters. Another little girl who comes by fairly frequently "flunked the first grade three times" and she still sits over in the sun on the left side of the room with those of her educational level. To this group of hopelessly uninspired children, driven only by whatever inherent personal curiosity they might be lucky enough to possess, Mrs. Zigos teaches spelling, reading, English, mathematics, geography, and "some health."

The second- and third-graders were taking turns reading from a book. Their singsong voices, almost inaudible murmers, did not do justice to the rather unusual and exciting tale they were reading. It was about a boy named Jack who encountered a fantastic beanstalk, a giant, and other equally extraordinary adventures.

A pretty little brown-haired girl was reading aloud, her brow squeezed in concentration. The boy behind her listened carefully, following the place with his fingers in his book because he would be next. The first-graders across the room alternately yawned and burst into flurries of writing: *AAA, BBB, CCC.*

The reader's voice droned on: ". . . but when Jack gave his beans to his mother she throwed them out the winder."

The teacher managed a wide-eyed look of anticipation, and tried vainly to strike a spark of enthusiasm. "What will they do now?" she asked the class. "No money. No food."

The children gave her a bored look. Jack's temporary shortage of food and money was nothing to get excited over. Something would show up. Even children hear so much of that kind of talk on Stinking Creek that they are sick of it. No food? No money? That's the stuff of fairy tales? Not on Stinking Creek.

Jack's adventures grew more complicated. He wanted a gold harp. His very life was threatened. All in the timid, faltering singsong voices—like the echo of an auctioneer's chant. Jack at last survived his James-Bond-like adventure, and the books were clapped shut with a soggy thud.

"Wasn't that a good story?" the teacher asked.

Silence.

The teacher erased the words on the board and replaced them with some the children had had difficulty with while reading:

wonderful	treasures
beautiful	harp
hungry	beanstalk
castle	brought

Shady School is not an isolated case, a school of unusual inadequacy selected from among schools of better caliber. Shady School sits in the center of the long middle stretch of Stinking Creek, along which live the Millses, the Messers, and the Sizemores, the families that produce many of the self-sufficient members of Stinking Creek. They are the political and social leaders, and here a few houses are neat, painted, and well kept. Many of these homes do not reflect the absolute abandonment of hope encountered in the smaller offshoot hollows such as Browns.

The Millses and the Messers and the Sizemores provide the local constables, drive the school buses, run the stores, own most of the trucks and cattle, and plant the large, orderly gardens that bloom in the narrow bottoms. Some even live without the aid of welfare checks. But Shady School is their school; it is what the county has decreed for them; so this is where they send their children when school age arrives.

That is why some of the weary little girls and boys who sit dejectedly in Shady School for the nine long months of the learning season are scrubbed, bright-eyed, and eager—at first. But at length their faces become more and more masked with the frustration of the poorer children, a look of ageless-ness and resignation. The door of Shady School does not open onto an exciting world of knowledge and intellectual adventure. The door opens only onto a shabby room thick with the smell of defeat; a room that appears embarrassed by the few books that stand like intruders on the two short, un-painted shelves, far back in a corner behind the teacher's desk.

At noon there were recess and lunch. The boys fled up the dusty road to Ellis Messer's store for "pop" and cake; those who could not afford this luxury wolfed down the stale sandwiches they brought in paper sacks. Most of the girls brought their lunches, ate them hurriedly, then skipped outside to play in the sunshine.

Behind the school is a "playhouse," enclosed in a low wall of the acid-stained round red rocks from the creek. Sometimes the girls play here. But usually they sit on the stones, and sing. They sing hymns, and their thin, clear voices ring loudly in the fatalistic words of the songs that tell of all those who, through sin, have lost forever the joys of heaven.

Mrs. Zigos remained inside and listened as the plaintive voices echoed up and down the creek. "That's the only kind of songs they sing—church songs," she said. "They get mad at me because I don't know them all. They just like to sit and play at church and pretend they are reading from a book."

The little voices outside were increasing in volume as other girls joined the group. They all appeared to know the words of dozens of hymns by heart: *"I'm sorry, I never knew you. . . ."* The words were clear and sad.

Mrs. Zigos shook her head slowly. "They all go to church," she said. "That's about all the recreation there is. Some got television this year."

And while the girls gathered under a gnarled maple tree and sang, the boys wandered aimlessly back, a few releasing their waning energy by tossing stones at the sullen creek.

In winter, the children stay inside during this midday break. At the rear of the building is a tiny walled-off compartment containing an electric stove and refrigerator. Hot lunches, as they are called in the reports the county school officials laboriously compile, are prepared here. Mrs. Zigos believes there is opportunity here to strike a few blows for better health.

"The girls cook; they open cans and warm the food up. The boys go out and get the water, and then the girls wash the dishes," she said. "I believe they have enough to eat. We get the commodities—chicken, beef barbecue to put on buns, cheese, peas, green beans, pork and beans, apple sauce, peanut butter. But they've eaten so much of that commodity meat at home they're tired of it." Mrs. Zigos shook her head wearily. "Everything around here comes in cans—the chicken and all the meat."

But the things that come in cans keep the children from growing weak from hunger during their school day, which begins for some at seven thirty in the morning and ends at four in the afternoon.

The matter of health education leads one onto strange ground at Shady School. Mrs. Zigos does the best she can. She remembers what the textbooks said so recently when she was a student at Union College, and she also knows a great deal about the hollows in which she grew up.

She laughed, the soft inner laugh of a mountain woman, and her blue eyes were gay as she said, "I don't believe they have toothbrushes." She lowered her voice. "They chew tobacco—the girls, I mean. I said, 'Law, you pretty little girls chewing!' They just laughed at me. They think if their mothers can do it, they can do it. Their parents does it."

Mrs. Zigos began to straighten the papers on her desk as the children wandered back into the building for their afternoon bout with education. At the rear of the room a little girl approached shyly, keeping her head tilted down. A hand shot out with a tightly folded piece of ruled notebook paper. The child flashed a conspiratorial smile, and went quickly to her seat, without looking back.

Later, when the note was unfolded, it read:

"DEAR SIR
"How are you I dont no your name will you tell me your name them picture's that you take to day my teacher said that you wood put them in a book please give me a book of us.

> "your truly
> "Linda Sue"

And far down at the bottom of the page was one tiny word:

"Love."

There was no school at Shady on the fourth Tuesday in May. On that date, academic forays were suspended while the building was called upon to serve another vital role in the life of the community. Shady School is the polling place for the Sixth Precinct, and time had come for the residents of Stinking Creek to elect the men who have a voice in their political destiny.

The crowds came early. They stood on a rocky point up on the road and looked solemnly down at the ancient school; they gathered in knots in the few shady places down by the creek and stared up at the school. Clark Sizemore, young and muscular, the constable, guarded the door, admitting the voters one at a time as they came quietly in from the bright sunshine to exercise the unique right of a free people upon the metallic, squat machine that recorded their choices.

Throughout the knots of people, those who "electioneered" for kin or friends passed back and forth, shook hands, spoke softly, and smiled . . .

and explained the forms that many must sign before they voted. The seriousness Clark Sizemore assumed as he guarded the portal to democracy and the
earnestness of those explaining the tiny paper forms were, in part, results of
what had happened four years ago at Shady School during an election. That
time it was a general election, held during one of the brilliant-hued Novem-
bers that bathe Stinking Creek in the crimson and gold of fall foliage.

But now one voted in a time when the Democrats were growing in power
under the influence of streams of cash being pumped from Washington and
Frankfort to douse the fires of poverty. And the Republicans, standing as
steadfastly as they could against the inundation of dollars, sought to cling
to their leadership as they muttered, "You can't beat Santa Claus."

Democrats and Republicans alike were determined that the fiasco of four
years ago would not be repeated. In that earlier election, Democrats were
elected, then unseated after a court battle. It all came about over a Kentucky
law that decrees that voters who cannot read and who require assistance
to flip the levers of the voting machine must sign an oath that "by inability
to read English . . . he is unable to vote without assistance."

In the voting, Mattie Mills, Hobert Mills, and Garret Brown, Democrats,
received the electorate's blessing for jailer, magistrate, and constable respec-
tively. But this was challenged, and in the court wrangle that followed, it
was argued that the oaths were not signed by those who were aided in the
polling place. A judgment to this effect was handed down in Knox Circuit
Court, then appealed to the state's highest court, the Kentucky Court of
Appeals. The high court affirmed the lower court's ruling. Thus Mattie Mills,
Hobert Mills, and Garrett Brown served only briefly in their posts of public
responsibility, and then were replaced by Lester Broughton, Henry Broughton, and Clark Sizemore, the Republicans.

With the full knowledge, then, that Stinking Creek's majority one way or
the other could swing a countywide election, an unusual seriousness was
apparent on the day the people of Stinking Creek came to vote.

Voter after voter cautiously approached the door, as though fully expect-
ing to be turned away. Every eye was on that door, and each voter came out
into the blazing glare of the sun and the more penetrating glare of his fellow citizens. And each voter shielded his own reactions from this intense
scrutiny with an expressionless mask he draws over his face at such times.

The linking of the ability to read and the right to vote is an annoyance
of great proportions to the people of Stinking Creek. The ability to read has
little to do with a man's ability to fell a tree, move a stone, or decide whom
he wants to dabble in the public funds as his duly elected servant.

In that contested election of 1961, it had developed that 68 of the 347 who voted at Shady School signed the comparative signature book with an *X*. And it was pointed out that half of all voters were assisted by the judges in making their choices on the voting machine. And none of the assisted voters had signed the oath. This time, they signed the oaths.

Hobert Mills, who had been knocked down by the court ruling after his election as magistrate, was back at the political wars as a candidate for jailer. Ellis Messer, Hobert's brother-in-law, was a candidate for magistrate, also on the Democratic ticket.

Both won that day in the sunshine at Shady School.

Hobert is known as a hustler. While he was in the magistrate's chair he got a few roads scraped off, and he supports a quiet, God-fearing family by gardening, operating a truck, and selling eggs and produce. If he should win the general election in November, he would move to the jailer's house in Barbourville and, for a time, find relief from the struggle of trying to survive on Stinking Creek.

Ellis Messer, who also manages to keep his mailbox free of relief checks, runs the store, drives a school bus, gardens, sometimes operates a small sawmill, and otherwise defies the economic facts of life on Stinking Creek.

Both men are regarded with considerable respect—if not outright awe—on Stinking Creek. There aren't many such "good hustlers" around.

On the day following the voting, Shady School again became a hall of learning. The beautiful children with their large trusting eyes and shy smiles returned. They returned to learn the lessons that will guide them someday when they, too, must help decide the political fate of their county.

By then, Jack and his outrageous beanstalk will be long forgotten. But the commodities and the checks probably will still be there—only, in more generous proportions. And the children who yawn and fret in the school today will carry on—as their parents now do—in the difficult pursuit of happiness on Stinking Creek.

8 The Young People

AFTER SHADY SCHOOL comes adolescence, on Stinking Creek as elsewhere, a difficult period. You are too old and too big to attend Shady School, and if you are qualified to attend high school you must ride the twenty miles to the county seat, and return, each day. Or you can discontinue your education. Primarily, you sit and wait—for what, you are never quite sure.

It is a restive, disquieting period of life, a time when you can get into trouble with the moonshine at a dollar a half pint or two dollars for boot-leg "red" bonded whiskey. And there are the dull-eyed loose girls ("Well, do you want some or not?"). Trouble is easy to find. Unless you have gotten religion. Fortunately, a goodly number of the young people on Stinking Creek have gotten religion.

Along the middle stretch of the creek, the best place for the boys to sit and wait for Fate to unfold her surprises is Ellis Messer's store. The store has fat sacks of cow feed to sit upon and a red electric cooler well stocked with king-sized soft drinks. With these comforts, waiting is almost tolerable.

If you sit upon the cow feed and drink pop long enough, you will meet most of the people on Stinking Creek. The store serves as community center, news center, and source of most things needed to sustain life. It is a small wooden building, soundly erected from heavy unfinished lumber that has weathered into a look of gray respectability with the changing seasons. The entrance, a solid board door, is in the center at the front, as are the two small windows, about two and a half feet square, which can let in the light during the summer and be sealed with their solid wooden shutters in the winter. A second door opens near the rear on the side toward Ellis Messer's comfortable white frame home. The store, the healthy garden behind it, the yellow school bus parked in front of the house, and a sawmill farther up Buckeye Fork attest to Ellis Messer's varied enterprises and solid standing

111

in the community. He is one of the few who make their own way on Stinking Creek.

When Ellis is driving his school bus or has gone to Barbourville on business, the store is run by his mall dark-haired wife or his twenty-two-year-old son, Kenneth. Ellis is a portly, contented man, and highly spoken of all up and down the creek. He cheerfully delivers the necessities of life to elderly people far up the remote hollows. "They ain't got no way in or out," he reasons. Ellis also extends credit freely.

The store, with Ellis in charge behind the rough counter and ancient brass scale, is a reassuring sight. It is the custom to stop by and trade with Ellis at least once a week if you live along that section of the creek.

The building is crammed with the good and necessary things of life. For those beset with infirmities of the body, there are Goody's Headache Powders, Bayer and St. Joseph aspirin, Syrup of Black-Draught, Red Cross Toothache kits, Pepto-Bismol, and small bottles of a clear liquid labeled "Isopropyl Rubbing Alcohol Compound, 70% Alcohol," which enjoys a steady demand.

Standing there facing Ellis and the largess on the unpainted wooden shelves behind him, an uncashed welfare check in your hand, the possibilities are intoxicating.

Stacked neatly and invitingly: Day's Work, Cut Plug, Apple, and Bull of the Woods chewing tobacco. Gladstone Cigars.

Delmonico Elbow Macaroni, Cheerios, 3-Minute Oats, Tall Boy Vegetable Soup, Kern's Sliced Bread, American Beauty Pork and Beans, Lykes Beef Stew in fat cans, Stokely's Orange Juice, Bush's Best White Hominy, Dixie Delite Yellow Freestone Peaches.

Toward the rear: flour in white bags and cornmeal in yellow bags.

It is time to shuffle your feet thoughtfully on the worn twelve-inch boards of the floor and ponder.

Candy bars: Payday, Hollywood, Zero, Milky Way, Loudy's Sugar Stick Candy.

White enameled steel racks loaded with cakes: Hostess Filled Sno-Balls, Snow-Cap Creme Pies, Bunny Jelly Sandwiches, Peanut Cremes. Purex in bilious green plastic bottles. Duz washing powders. Oilcloth, shiny white with red figures, seventy-four cents a yard cut from a fifty-four-inch roll. Men's white socks, thirty-nine and fifty cents. Brooms, their pristine bristles bright yellow.

Along the wall opposite the counter and the loaded shelves are the red cooler, a humming Frigidaire, and the bulging, brightly colored sacks of cow feed. The gay print cotton bags can be washed and made into dresses,

Road up Acorn Fork. The girl is Monica Mills, thirteen.

aprons, towels, and bonnets. Above the cow feed, nails hold shiny galvanized buckets, pans, and water dippers. A hundred-pound burlap sack of pinto beans, which have risen in price to two pounds for thirty-five cents. Inflation also has touched the sausage cooling in the Frigidaire. It is now fifty-five cents a pound, and a luxury to be purchased sparingly. Nails, gleaming in their brown boxes on the floor in front of the counter, are now fifteen cents a pound.

All this is temptingly in view as you settle onto a bag of cow feed at Ellis Messer's quick invitation to "stay and sit with us."

A bag of cow feed, if you are patient, makes an excellent seat. A bit uncomfortable at first, the crushed grains beneath the colorful cotton gradually shift and yield and at length form themselves into a restful contour that is both extremely personal and comfortable. The cow-feed bags also provide an unobstructed view of all that transpires in the store, and serve as a vantage point for greeting arrivals. They are the correct distance from the pot-bellied coal-burning stove in the center of the store. The hundred-pound feed bags—mustily aromatic contents, bright covering, and all—costs $3.65. It would take many times that much money to buy a chair more luxurious.

There on the stuffed feed bags, you meet and talk with the boys and young men. And watch the customers.

Entering and trading at Ellis Messer's store is an unvarying ritual. You step up from the dusty road and into the comparative gloom of the interior and nod to the men and boys reclining on the cow-feed bags. Then you walk directly to the bright red Coca-Cola cooler squatting against the wall. You always have a pop first. If children come along, they walk silently to the cooler and await the signal to reach in.

Pop flows freely on Stinking Creek. Youth drink eight or ten bottles a day. The tiniest youngster can gulp down a king-size bottle in minutes. The selection is a thoughtful and unhurried decision. You lift one large hinged lid and peer inside. Diet Rite, Dr. Pepper, Tab, Mountain Dew. You drop the lid, lift the other lid and examine the contents of the other half of the cooler. Seven-Up, Coca-Cola, Grape, Orange. The crimped top of the pop bottle is lifted on an opener nailed to the wall; the top clatters into a cardboard box on the floor, and the customer takes a deep, long pull from the bottle. Then, accompanied by his silent children, he walks over to examine the delicacies on the metal bakery shelf. "Have a cake if you want," the head of the house says. Like flickers of spring lightning, young fingers snatch the cookies and cakes from their resting place and tear off the clear plastic covers. The craving for the sting of carbonated beverages and the lingering sweetness of the little cakes and assorted fruit bars is constant.

Messer's store, with Ellis Messer in the doorway

Messer's store, with Ellis Messer behind the counter.
This photograph was taken on "check day."

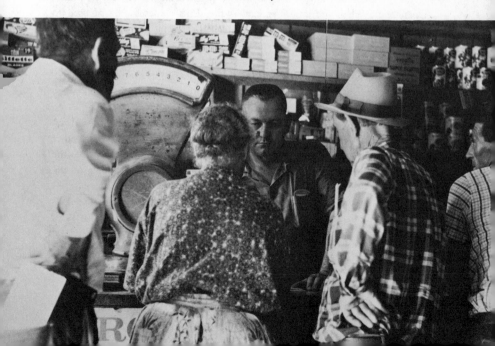

A first reaction, as you sit on the feed bags and watched the performance day after day, is, "Why do they waste money on that junk?"

The answer is clear when you stay long on Stinking Creek. A bland diet—green beans and cabbage in the summer. Fried pork, corn bread, black coffee. Meal after meal. Surplus-commodity meat—pork and beef—extracted from its shiny cans and fried in bubbling lard grease in black frypans. "Taters" swimming in clear grease. Adequate, but all blandness and grease. It leaves a disturbing unfilled sensation, a nagging, evasive hunger. Tobacco won't satisfy it. But pop and cake will—for a time. Ellis Messer sometimes sells fifty cases of pop a week; eight cents if you drink it in the store, ten cents if you carry the bottle out. The empties present a constant problem, and they are stacked around the stove and outside on the ground on either side of the door.

The biggest trading day in Ellis Messer's store is on check day when the dollars sent to fight poverty come pouring in. Crisp, heavy paper checks, perforated to be processed by electronic machines later in Washington or the state capital. The checks protrude proudly from the shirt pockets of the men and burn impatiently in the apron pockets of the women. Check day is the day to pay up last month's credit that has been carefully added and double-checked by Ellis. Messer.

Ellis keeps his records in a worn blue looseleaf notebook, and each page represents a customer on credit. Purchases are entered with a heavy pencil. When you pay up, Ellis adds the figures, takes the welfare check, and subtracts the amount needed to restore the customer to debt-free independence. When the customer can't write, Ellis witnesses the X used to endorse the check. As he hands the change over, Ellis pulls the customer's page from the notebook, ceremoniously folds it into a small square, and hands it over. "You might check that when you get time," he says. "If I made a mistake you know where you got it." The figures are rarely checked, for two reasons. Folks on Stinking Creek trust Ellis Messer, and many customers can't read the rows of numbers anyway.

With pop and cake consumed and last month's credit disposed of, the time to trade has come. Ellis and his customer regard each other unblinkingly across the counter: the customer silent and studying the shelves; Ellis solemn and waiting, one arm resting on the pan of the ancient scale.

The trading is time-consuming, deliberate, and deadly serious. The conversation is brief and to the point, and for a time gossip and matters of less import are put aside.

"You got flour?"

"Plain or self-rising?"

A pause for reflection, as though there might be a remote chance that on some eventful day the self-rising might be selected. "Give me a sack of plain."

Ellis fetches the flour in its white bag and enshrines it on the counter between himself and the customer.

"Got ary cornmeal?"

"Yep."

"Two sacks."

The yellow paper sacks are brought to the counter and hefted into place beside the flour.

"Got ary light bread?"

"Got Kern's sliced."

"Give me a cake of that."

The bread joins the selected groceries on the counter.

"You got lard?"

"It's went up five cents."

A pause, while the customer studies the pastoral illustration on the Commonwealth Life Insurance Company calendar on the front wall.

"Two boxes."

The staples are taken care of first—always the flour, cornmeal, lard, and pork side meat, a white, salted chunk of meat wrapped in a brown paper that quickly absorbs the grease. The pile of groceries grows steadily. The trading pace slows as the customer carefully regards his accumulated purchases piled reassuringly on the counter between the two men like a monument to the astuteness of the buyer. The customer rocks slowly on his heels and lets his eyes play over the groceries he has bought, measuring the provisions against the demands of the young uns at home, the remains of his welfare check, and the length of time until the next check will be deposited in his mailbox.

The customer moves cautiously from the field of necessity into the treacherous area of luxury. He glances down at his children standing quietly beside him, their bright, wide eyes straining to see upon the high counter. The provider reads a plea in their young faces. Prudence is swept aside by a swell of love and of pride. There ought to be something a man can do for the young uns.

The customer looks at his children a few moments, then turns solemnly to Ellis. "You got Kool Aide?"

"Got the sweetened kind. What flavor you like?"

"Strawberry," the man says, checking his selection with a quick downward glance. The laughing eyes of his brood confirm the decision.

Ellis has his pencil in his hand, but he has not yet turned to the customer's place in the blue looseleaf notebook. He knows the trading is not yet completed.

The customer hesitates, and hooks his thumbs into the bib of his overalls. Ellis waits patiently. He knows the struggle going on in the man's mind and how it will end. It is check day. The old woman and the young uns have been good this month. Hell, a man's got to do what he can for his own kind. And do it while he can, because he might not be able to do for them tomorrow.

The customer walks over to a lone angel-food cake. Its sticker says fifty-nine cents. The man hefts it, walks erectly back to the counter past his adoring children, and places the cake on top of the groceries.

"How much is that?" he asks,

"Fifty-nine cents," Ellis confirms.

"Put it down, too."

Ellis knows the trading is done. He opens the notebook and begins the meticulous entry of the purchases against next month's check.

The trading is ignored by the men and boys who shift their weight on the cow-feed sacks, and talk. They appear unaware of the constant trading at the counter a few feet away—unless a customer wants a sack of cow feed. Then they rise while Ellis or his boy, Kenneth, drags a sack from the pile and carries it out to be hoisted onto the back of a mule or into a car or pickup truck. The men and boys settle back immediately, and although sack after sack disappears during the day, the number of available seats appears to decrease only slowly. When the supply of cow-feed seats dwindles to almost nothing, upended soft-drink cases are pressed into service.

The cow-feed sacks are a pleasant place to sit, and the store has a warm earthy smell of seasoned wood and people. In winter, the black stove gurgles defiance at the howling weather, and in summer drafts of cool air sometimes fan through the store.

The boys and men talk of hunting, of dogs, of things they have seen on the mountain that rises skyward behind the store. They talk and gossip and wink at the children who come in, and chide the old people. There is an unfailing and sincere respect for old people on Stinkng Creek. The young boys laugh and joke with them, but their laughter is never of derision; rather it is like fond chuckling at an errant child.

So when spry Aunt Louisa Sizemore comes in pertly and orders her trading goods in authoritative and certain tones, the boys laugh at Ellis

Messer's quick compliance, and tell her, "You'll never eat all that, Aunt Louisa."

Louisa Sizemore is ninety-nine. "At least that's what I think I am," she says.

When there are no customers and all the welfare checks have been safely deposited in the wooden cash drawer, Ellis leans on the counter and listens to the young men talk. He grew up in the hollow and has heard the stories many times, but he always listens and shows appropriate wonder at each repeated tale.

"Snakes is the worst at berrypicking time. They'll sit in the bushes, and sometimes you can't even hear a rattlesnake singing. A woman in Clay County got eat up by them. She was picking huckleberries when they hit her, and they counted forty rattlesnakes on her."

"I had this little dog, and she killed every snake she seen. I heard one singing down in the creek, and pretty soon she come out with it. Man, she was wearing it out along the creek bottom, carrying that snake. She was bit in the back, but she had that snake. She killed it and it killed her. I seen it was too late to help her."

"I heered some things on this mountain would scare you. I heered some creature singing, and even the best dog I got heered it and turned down the mountain. He knowed something about whatever it was singing that night. I tell you I had my shotgun, but I never went no closer to find out what it was. I just as soon not find out.

"I just as soon not find out everything that's on these mountains. I know where Indian graves are, and that's about all that's up there."

"I know where some Indian springs are. The rocks are all smoothed out. Just as smooth as you please."

"I run into an old man up there, and he said he knowed where a gold mine was, but he didn't have enough sense to know the war was over."

The last observation was rewarded with a round of laughter, and several boys volunteered that they had run into the old man wandering up on the mountain. "There ain't no diamond or gold mines in this country. It's rich in rocks," a boy said.

The others nodded agreement, and a muscular youth added: "The Indians knowed what they was about. They left this country to the white man. They said, 'If you knowed what it's like around this country, you'd shoe your horses and go right on.' "

"Well, there's black walnut which brings good money—only there ain't none left now, I reckon."

"There ain't nothing, just rocks."

"Why couldn't there be something else? They've got coal and gas out of these mountains."

But the optimistic element was silenced by the more practical observers of the contemporary scene on Stinking Creek.

"Only thing we got in these parts is some things I don't know what they are. I been in caves where you'd get scared of yourself."

"Buddy, you're just scared of yourself."

"You better be scared of some things."

"Well, we got some rabbits and a sick squirrel or two."

"And we got yaller root. That's good for upset stomach or ulcers."

The last speaker was Ben Smith, a stout boy in his early twenties. A few days later he married Aileen Mills, a slender brown-haired girl who lived down by Laurel Fork, and moved north—to find himself a city and a job and a place where you don't have to take yaller root for ulcers.

The boys are lithe and strong and courteous. Gobel Mills, Junior, is straight and slender, and has thick black hair combed up and away from a lean brown face. He's always ready to rough it up with the strongest youth or gently horseplay with a small boy. There is Harold Bargo, shaking his unruly fiery red hair, waving and calling when he spots you from a distance, a youth who knows everybody—and likes everybody on Stinking Creek. Kenneth Messer, small like his mother, joins the boys on the feed sacks, but takes over the store when his parents are gone, selling the pop and the meal and the lard and making meticulous entries in the blue notebook. Jim Tom Blankenship, heavy and muscular and quiet, has the body of a football player and a surprising fondness for singing in a gentle baritone voice. Bill Cox, tall and smooth-muscled, with dark features and complexion, listens quietly, and smiles when other eyes meet his. All these, and many more, sit waiting and hoping on the feed sacks at Ellis Messer's store.

All the boys have a fondness for pop and old cars. An old car is something you can touch and know is yours. You can buy one for as little as $50, and spend the summer laboring under the hood and flat on the ground, straining at the grimy parts beneath the jalopy's battered belly. There are few boys on Stinking Creek who cannot tune and adjust a gasoline motor, bleed and adjust brakes, and do makeshift repairs with bits of wire and hose and steel.

And you can race the ancient vehicles up and down the gravel road, sending a choking blanket of dust across the countryside. The coughing growl of pitted cylinders, the staccato of gravel hurled by spinning wheels as it rips through roadside foliage and into dented fenders. It is a dangerous sport; occasionally one will lose control and plunge off the narrow, winding road. But usually they are lucky, and the thick undergrowth and oak and redwood saplings along the shoulder of the road will cushion and check the velocity of the hurtling car before it crashes into a vine-shrouded boulder. Then a neighbor with a truck will happen along and pull the car back onto the road with a rusty logging chain for only a dollar or two. If Wade Smith and his International flatbed truck are around, you'll get pulled out for free. Wade, as anybody knows, is "a right good feller."

After it's all over, and the tangled weeds have been pulled from the bumpers and the fenders kicked free of contact with the bald tires, there is something different to laugh and talk about back at Ellis Messer's store . . . over a pop.

You can sit in Messer's store, out on the creek bank, or in the shade of Salem Baptist Church and talk forever with the young men of Stinking Creek—and always get the same answers:

They don't blame their fathers or their grandfathers for any of their hardships.

They don't want to leave, but are afraid that someday they must.

They know, and are candid about, the strengths and weaknesses of the people about them.

On a humid day, when intermittent rains were keeping the dust settled, a dozen or so boys sat and talked. They moved inside the old stone Messer school to escape the showers. All the boys were eager to see that, as one boy put it, "You git down exactly what our true feelin's are so there won't be no mistake about that, buddy."

Tell me how the people here really are:

"Some are hoggish—the Gospel truth. Some are greedy. Some say, 'If I live at the mouth of a holler, I don't care about the people up at the head of the holler.' It's like a tradition. They won't change their ways. When they get a road to their house, they're satisfied. They won't give a right of way past there."

"Well, sir, if they'd ever had anything before, they'd most likely be more generous."

"In one way they are smart as anybody you'd care to meet; in one way, the dumbest you can get."

"They have the least worries. They don't worry if they're working."

"Oh, the people is intelligent. The officials get the money, but people around here don't see their share. Everybody'll tell you the officials bottle it up."

"The old people ain't willing to change. It's all been handed down through the generations. The old people won't even answer the surveys. They think you're raising taxes or cutting them off the welfare."

"That may be right. But I don't know a family from the mouth of Middle Fork to the head of this creek but what would help if anybody asked."

"The people are hospitable. You saw for yourself they're willing to feed you."

What's good and bad about Stinking Creek?

"You got better air to breathe and better water than they got in the cities."

"You ain't always hemmed up."

"Not all that smoke and fumes."

"Quieter. I seen Detroit. Here, you don't stay awake all night from cars."

"If I didn't have my own old cow, I'd die. It wouldn't seem right to sit down without your own milk."

"But how many people you think got milk? Just a couple between here and Buckeye Fork."

"We don't have to rush here and rush there. We got time to go fishing and swimming—only now the creek burns your eyes with that acid."

"This place is going to be better. I understand the government is going to spend a lot of money. We already lost a steam plant and some factories. We'd stay right here rest of our days if we had something to work at."

"I hate to go lookin' for work. If I ever had a good teacher in my life, I can't call her to mind."

"I haven't had none, either."

"I think I had one good teacher as far back as I can remember."

"All I went for was recess and dinner. Some'd go all week to play ball on Friday evening. Their parents never went to school. They don't know the value of going to school. And nobody can make you go."

"You get so far behind you're ashamed to go. I got to the seventh grade, and they passed me just to get me out of the way."

"Some teachers left here to teach school in Ohio. It pays them better wages."

"I think they are just robbing the children when they send us bad teachers."

What about the welfare?

"Some grownups are on the checks because they don't know how to manage."

"Well, I'm one that don't like the commodities."

"People will complain about the commodities, but if they turn up short one bean they holler."

"Some feeds the commodities to the hogs."

"We made Spanish rice out of the commodities, like they showed us to, and it looked like slop."

"Well, honey, I ain't going to live on the welfare. I may be in Chicago, but when I get my own family I sure ain't going to be on the welfare."

What about jobs?

"Folks are getting wore out begging for jobs."

"The jobs are in Detroit and Chicago. About everybody around here's been there and back."

"You find a job in Barbourville, and it won't even pay transportation there and back."

"You see, in the city it's root, hog, or die."

"Well, in the city they at least got something to root at."

"Will you stay on Stinking Creek—or leave?"

"When you get to be a married man, you can't stay around here."

"The men working, they say: 'This is just old government work. I don't have to work very hard.' That ain't the right way to look at it."

"Most are getting too used to welfare and social security, and they won't never leave."

"I'd work at anything to stay right on this creek. But I don't think it's true with the girls—they'd rather be in the city."

"I know a lot of people would give a million dollars to get back on Stinking Creek."

On a hot, airless Monday morning, three of the young men rounded up three power mowers and a glass jug of gasoline and loaded it all in Messer's old blue pickup truck. They were stripped to the waist and already sweating under the white sun. "Goin' to clean the cemetery," one of them shouted as they disappeared behind a wall of white dust churned up from the dry gravel road.

The little cemetery where the Mills and Messer dead lie is atop a rounded knoll that arches high above a long bend in the creek. A wire fence protects it from straying livestock, but not from the encroachment of vines, Johnson grass, and weeds. The undergrowth was dry from days of rainless sunshine, and it appeared to disintegrate into a dust under the

*Gobel Mills, Jr., left, and Kenneth Messer
cleaning the cemetery*

roaring mowers, a powdery residue that floated and hung in the air and settled on the sweating backs of the three workers.

The three—Kenneth Messer, Gobel Mills, Jr., and Jim Tom Blankenship—worked for an hour without pausing, charging the mowers at the tangled underbrush and sometimes tearing it away from the bases of the grave markers with their bare hands. Then they stopped to rest. And one was sent back to the store for pop. Refreshed, they returned to the task, and within a few hours the little cemetery was neat and trimmed. And most of the inscriptions were again visible.

The three young men sat in the shade, panting and perspiring.

"Lot of our kin here," Kenneth said.

There were. For a long, long time, the dead of the Mills and Messer families have been carried to this point of the knoll above the creek, buried and preached and wept over, and finally marked with a stone and an inscription.

Euphemia Mills Carnes, "Asleep in Jesus." Rosa Mills Warfield, who drowned, "Weep Not Father and Mother for Me." T. J. and Emma Mills, "Gone but Not Forgotten." Little Martha Wilson, who was born on New Year's day in 1892 and died before she was three months old, "Budded on Earth to Bloom in Heaven." Toward the front of the cemetery, the newer graves. John H. Mills, "He Has Gone to the Mansions of Rest." Lee Roy Mills, "Prepare to Meet Me in Heaven."

It took several bottles of pop back at Messer's store to bring complete recovery from the labor of clearing out the cemetery. But completion of the job brought a noticeable feeling of well-being.

The boys of the Mills and Messer families, and those kin to them, want to be buried someday in that little cemetery perched above the bend in Stinking Creek. Not in Detroit or Chicago.

If there were a soda fountain on Stinking Creek, Peggy Mills would have gone there. Instead, she came into Messer's store. Peggy ignored the boys lounging on the feed sacks and walked directly to the Frigidaire. She took out a huge roll of bologna and carried it over to the counter. Ellis plopped an already opened loaf of bread on the counter and turned to fetch a half-full jar of Shedd's Salad Dressing and a huge butcher knife.

Peggy sliced an inch-thick slab from the bologna with the big knife and spread two pieces of bread with the salad dressing. She ate the monstrous sandwich daintily, nodding an affirmative answer when Ellis politely asked, "You all right today, Peggy?"

Ellis sells oversized bologna sandwiches for twenty-five cents, and you

Peggy Mills in Messer's store,
with Mrs. Ellis Messer behind the counter

make them yourself. It's a good thing to know when you are that far up Stinking Creek and don't have an invitation to dinner.

Peggy Mills, maturing swiftly at sixteen, the still-changing slender legs of childhood and the full breasts of womanhood. Eating a hugh bologna sandwich and waiting, as all the young people wait, for a future. Thick, long dark-brown hair that is always well cared for, and wide hazel eyes that seem to change color—from hazel to blue to green—to complement the changing colors around them. Peggy is still a child, but not a child. A young woman, but not yet a young woman.

She has a soft, breathy mountain accent: "I ought to brush my hawr if you're fixin' to take my pitchure."

Peggy lives in a neat white frame house within sight of Stinking Creek. In front of her home, Acorn Fork runs its final yards before being swallowed up by the larger creek. Her family is one of the oldest and most respected along the creek.

Jim Mills, who came from North Carolina, was the first Mills to see Stinking Creek. And he left a large, God-fearing, hard-working "generation." "Nabe" Mills, Peggy's grandfather, runs the store and is the postmaster at Mills, Kentucky, which consists of the combination store and post office and Nabe's big two-story house. Peggy's father is Hobert Mills, who won the Democratic primary for jailer. The primary was a big day for Peggy. If Hobert had won the general election later, he would have moved Peggy and her mother into Barbourville to live in the drab brick jailer's house. Unlike the boys, Peggy was eager to leave Stinking Creek.

Acorn Fork and Stinking Creek were splendid playgrounds for Peggy the little girl. But they are a prison for Peggy the big girl. Sometimes she puts on her bathing suit and walks over to splash in the creek, but now she is self-conscious. "I declare, it just don't seem to be fun anymore. Daddy's old-timey. He said he didn't want boys coming around here."

Hobert Mills is, perhaps, "old-timey." He also is considered to be somewhat of a go-getter. Four times he has been elected magistrate of Knox County's Fourth District. Once was the time when the legal wrangling broke out over the voters who got help at the machines and did not sign the required oaths. Hobert also has worked for the State Highway Department, operates a truck, and raises vegetables, chickens, and cows. As a result of these exertions, his family has universal respect and inside plumbing.

Peggy rides the bus into Barbourville to attend high school, and this brings her into contact with an element of city life that returns her admiration—boys.

"I sure do like the boys in town," she said. "The boys in town know how to treat you. They got better manners, you know. They're prettier, too."

She is completely unimpressed by the boys on Stinking Creek. "We got some here, but all the cute ones I'm kin to."

She is a mine of information on "the boys in town." "Why, they open a door for you. They ask you what time you have to be home. The boys in town, you can tell them you can't do certain things. The boys in town will walk you to the door when you get home."

She is a bit peeved at any defense of the local boys. She arched a dark eyebrow and said with some defiance, "Your boys out here could improve some."

Peggy says many of the boys at school talk to her. She is not the kind of girl a teen-age boy passes up without a second glance. "They all end up talking about cars," she said. "They all talk about cars. I like to talk about life—like when we were little. I like to hear scary tales and have scary dreams."

Peggy said she doesn't remember ever going to a young people's party on Stinking Creek. "The boys just stay at the store, and gossip." It isn't considered proper for girls to use the store for a hangout. So Peggy, during the long summer school vacation, suns herself in the backyard, with an occasional cooling splash from a nearby bucket of water. Or she helps with the housework. She likes to wash and "owrn" her own clothes.

Peggy is a good student. She got *A*'s in typing and biology, *B*'s in English and home economics, and slipped to a *D* in algebra. "When I get out of high school I want to go to college because I want a good job—really good. I think I want to teach."

She teaches a Sunday-school class of fifteen tots at Salem Baptist Church. Peggy attends there regularly and sings in the choir. When asked to tell exactly what she wants out of life, she answers:

"I'd like to get married when I'm twenty-one. I want a Christian husband and one that'll work and has been to college. I want a set of encyclopedia books. That's what I've had in mind to get for a good long time. And I'd like to live in Michigan . . . in Detroit."

While most of the young people are restive, others perhaps could live out their lives in the mountains free from the vague goading frustrations that beset their peers. J. Harold Sizemore and his sister, Virginia, are two such young people.

On a warm Sunday morning J. Harold announced, as usual, that he

Peggy Mills

Peggy Mills—she's "kin to all the cute boys"

J. Harold Sizemore

was too busy to go to preaching. So he sat by the side of the gravel road across from the point where Alex Creek tumbles acid mine water into Stinking Creek, and watched a mutilated possum.

"My name is J. Harold Sizemore," he said. "J. Harold Sizemore." He said it twice because he likes the sound of it.

"The J. comes first," he said.

A name with an initial that comes first is one of J. Harold's most prized possessions. It is a distinction denied most people on Stinking Creek. Along with the J. that comes first, J. Harold has an eighth-grade education, a sharp pocket knife, and a swarm of nondescript dogs reasonably suitable for hunting or trading. All of which makes life as full as J. Harold can envision. At seventeen, he is happy and busy.

He had been distracted from being busy watching the creek bubble by when one of his dogs noisily cornered the possum against a rocky corner of the creek bank. When J. Harold came to investigate, the possum feigned death. J. Harold took out his pocket knife and neatly severed the possum's ears. The possum lay motionless, still heeding an erroneous instinct to lie motionless and thereby escape harm.

J. Harold cleaned his knifeblade on a broad pokeberry leaf, returned it to his pocket, and silently observed the possum. "I reckon he's hurtin' some with his ears cut off," he said.

J. Harold was a study in concentration as he squatted and watched the animal, as though some great truth were to be learned from its behavior. A lanky youth with pale blue eyes, brown hair, and sallow complexion despite countless hours spent hunting and wandering, he wore denim pants, low-top "loafer" shoes, a colorless jacket over a khaki shirt, and a plastic hat with the brim turned up all the way round.

People began to walk by on the road. Church was breaking, J. Harold observed, and it was well attended by those who, unlike J. Harold, could spare the time to attend. "I don't never hardly go myself," J. Harold said. "When I got time I run my dogs. I got one dog, just a cur, can outrun any beagle on this creek. It would take $50 to buy any dog I got."

Since Harold's mother and thirteen-year-old sister, Virginia, attend the Holiness Church regularly, Harold sometimes goes down and sits in the sun outside during the preaching. "I'm just knockin' about," he said. "I don't never go in much. It lasts three hours."

J. Harold waved a long arm toward the mountain in front of the church. "I already walked all over yander mountain this morning. Never seen a groundhog." He gave the motionless possum a look of contempt. "A groundhog will run and turn and jump right at you. Buddy, you jump a groundhog you got to mind how you act. Jump right at you, and hiss. Scared o' nothin'."

The dispensing of this information seemed to tire J. Harold. He squatted back on his lean haunches to recapture his strength. "I'm just knockin' about," he said. "Ain't goin' nowhere for certain. You ever seen a groundhog? I can take them dogs and git you one pretty quick."

A week or so later, J. Harold did go on a groundhog hunt. A light snow had melted, and the ground was muddy and treacherous. J. Harold and a friend, fourteen-year-old Ronald Patterson, whistled up a pack of six nondescript dogs, kicked them toward the mountain behind J. Harold's house, and started climbing. The mountain rose sharply, but the two boys moved up it with a long-legged, effortless grace, leaning slightly forward and taking long strides that carried them quickly to a level place several hundred feet above Stinking Creek. Here, they paused to rest.

J. Harold produced a can of Prince Albert tobacco, and the boys rolled cigarettes while the dogs slumped to the ground around them. J. Harold's hunting dogs, in which he takes great pride, were not in a hunting mood.

"It looks like they just want to lay and waller," J. Harold said. Then he barked out the dogs' names in quick order, "Rover! Copsie! Yaller! Sport! Brownie! Sparky!" The dogs came slowly to life, then scampered off to survey the game situation under a hail of stones hurled by the two boys. Except Yaller. Older and wiser than the others, he scampered a few feet away, collapsed behind a log, yawned luxuriously, and dozed off.

J. Harold lolled back on one elbow and expertly rolled another cigarette. Hold the tissue-thin paper in the left hand between thumb and second finger, the forefinger on top to make the paper form a long, slender trough. Shake the tilted Prince Albert can gently until a mound of shredded tobacco lies in the center of the curved paper. Pass the flat red can on to the next man. Spread the tobacco evenly along the paper with the forefinger of the right hand, lick the furthermost edge of the paper, and roll it tightly, using the thumb and first two fingers of either hand. Crimp the ends to hold the tobacco. Light it. A rich, heavy blue smoke drifts flatly beneath the forest canopy.

This was one of J. Harold's busy days and one of the reasons he has no time for school. "I went through the eighth grade. I don't guess I'll ever go back thar. I'm undecided, you might say." He let his thoughts wander as he looked down from his vantage point on the mountain. "This is just a mountain. I don't know if it's got ary name. Got no timbers left. Got some hazelnuts left."

He doesn't care for steady jobs. "I worked in the deep mines oncet. They would get the coal shot down, and we went in and loaded. After I quit it fell in. I only worked about two weeks, and I don't care to go back inside no mountain."

He pointed to the east. "Man over there had the diabetes. He got drunk and got his sugar stirred up. They cut off his leg and he died."

J. Harold seemed pleased that his reporting of such well-known events along Stinking Creek was of any interest. He wrinkled his brow as he tried to think of something else of equal importance. "I don't git up 'til ten on a Sunday when I ain't got nothing to do," he said. "Some Sundays I got things to do. Run the dogs. Go to the head of the holler and box around with a friend."

His friend at the head of the hollow is Donald North, a handsome blond of sixteen who lives in the last house up near the spongy place that is the source of Stinking Creek.

"Me and Donald, we just cut up and talk," J. Harold said. "Donald's still a-goin' to school. Donald's folks got another little old two-room house, just two beds and a heating stove. Me and Donald we stay there a lot and pillow fight and talk about the girls. I ain't got one. I just talk about 'em. We pillow fight in the dark. You never know when one is going to hit you. They ain't really pillows. More like old couch cushions. One hit my jaw and like to broke it. I spent nearly every night one week up there just talking and pillow fighting."

He told about his family's mule. "We give $165 for her and she's ten year old," J. Harold said. "She eats a $2.35 sack of corn every two weeks, and a bale of hay costs fifty cents to a dollar. She can eat one of them in about a week. First year we didn't have no fodder of our own. Now we'll raise corn and we'll put up some fodder for this winter. Boy! Don't never buy no mule in the spring of the year. They'll break you up."

He let his eye sweep the panorama below to see if there was anything else of local note to report, but could find nothing. The dogs were beginning to wander back, eying J. Harold tentatively. Two of them growled and snapped at each other, and J. Harold said: "That Rover. Grouchiest old dog I ever seen. Any dogs gets around, he wants to jump all over them." J. Harold sent a rock thudding into the dog's side, and the entire pack fled to resume its hunting responsibilities.

"I like to see a dog and a groundhog a-fightin'. That's the best fight you ever did see," J. Harold said. The lack of activity from the dogs was becoming a bit embarrassing, and J. Harold explained, "I allowed my dogs'd already jumped at least a rabbit by now."

A dog yelped about three hundred yards away and higher up on the mountain. J. Harold and Ronald leaped to their feet running, Ronald carrying a battered, heavy mattock. When they reached the baying dogs, Rover and Sparky were frantically barking canine insults into a small hole in the ground. The other dogs sat down to watch this actively with some disgust.

"He's in there," J. Harold said. "That Rover's got him."

Harold broke off a poplar sapling about six feet long, jerked the dogs roughly away from the hole, and jabbed the stick into it. When he felt the stick touch something, he twisted it, jabbed harder, twisted it and withdrew it. The jagged end of the stick brought out a few gray hairs. J. Harold studied the hairs. Felt them. Smelled them. "Them's groundhog hairs," he said.

J. Harold seized the two dogs and hurled them at the hole to show them their action stations. While the two dogs yelped into the hole, J. Harold began digging into the moist earth about six feet above the hole, digging steadily and strongly, the heavy mattock rising and falling rhyhmically. "We'll break in on it about here," he said.

But he hit a large rock that took thirty minutes to extract from the clinging earth. Then, Ronald, taking a turn with the mattock, hit an even larger rock. The two boys alternated with the mattock, panting and flailing at the solid rock. As one dug, the other kept up a constant stream of heckling.

"You're bound to lose a hand, ain't you?"

"Heave that rock out. No, over on this here side."

When the rusty mattock head flew off, J. Harold quickly repaired it, fashioning a wedge from a small stick with his pocket knife. The boys dug and searched for ways around the big rock. But the groundhog was in an impregnable fortress. At last, panting and exhausted after nearly two hours of digging, they gave up.

The defeat was bitter. "I wanted to catch me some baby ones and train them," J. Harold said. "I had a gray squirrel last year, and he died on me."

Before the boys started back down the mountain, J. Harold gave the hole a final savage poke with the long poplar stick, and muttered, "If I could get to it, I'd cut its ears off."

When J. Harold gets home, he is the man of the family. His father has left for Harlan County, where he stays most of the time, and Mary Sizemore, J. Harold's mother, struggles with the upbringing of J. Harold and the six other young Sizemores still at home.

Her marriage lasted twenty-two years, and Mary is not yet fully adjusted to the full responsibility of running her crowded, small mountain home. She sits in the rocker in her front room, a woman of forty, her face like the hills around her, naturally attractive but abused by fate. On her lap, one-year-old Robert laughed, slapped at her, tugged at her dress in a constant squirming of young enthusiasm. Mrs. Sizemore was tired. She rocked slowly and sadly, watching the white dust clouds, churned up by a black Pontiac that had just passed by, settling slowly.

"I don't know what I've got into," she said. "Me and him, we was married twenty-two years. We had nine young uns. One, she died with rheumatic heart; one boy is married and gone." She rocked slowly. All the family was there in the room, warmed by a sulfurous coal fire in the fireplace: Virginia, thirteen, pale, blonde, attractive, her hair long and uncut "because she belongs to God and won't never cut it no more now"; J. Harold and the smaller Sizemores, Jimmy, fifteen; Kenneth, eleven; Michael, nine; and Bill, four, named for his father.

A gray room, a yellow light from the fire, and a bluish-white reflected light from the wintry hills. A large bed, the rocker, a worn blue over-stuffed chair, a dresser, a baby bed, the children's extra clothing hung from nails near the fireplace. And a television set showing a movie rerun, gangsters and cops battling in a big-city setting. The children sat on the bed and watched or occasionally strayed into one of the other two rooms that serve as bedrooms, or into the kitchen at the rear, a room perched high on the hillside on stout posts.

Mrs. Sizemore is neater and friendlier than most of the thousands of mountain women caught in similar circumstances. Her dark-brown hair was gathered into a tight bun on top of her head, held by long pins, the protruding pinheads decorated with bits of shell. She wore a loose brown dress and high-top fur-lined house shoes.

"I wasn't but eighteen when we got married," she said. "He was loading coal then. Things looked good. We lived in a pretty good place up the next holler when Harold was born. But he got a spite for me. Seems like he wants to live with his people over in Harlan County. Some men take a notion to go. They just up and gone."

The children, whenever one passed by, poked playfully at the baby, and each time the baby would turn, grab eagerly at the tormenter, and gurgle ecstatically.

Mary was still thinking of the husband she had had for twenty-two years. "He acknowledges he's guilty. He gives me $70 a month. He's working and makes $18 a shift. The kids are all big eaters. Lord, they eat big. All they can get. It takes a lot of money. Seems like I can't do no good. Just $70 a month ain't no money."

Of the $70 a month Mrs. Sizemore gets from her husband, she pays $12 a month rent for the house, and "my juice runs over $4 a month." The electricity is the only utility she has to pay. Water comes from a well, and heat from the open fireplaces and the bits of coal and wood she burns in her kitchen stove.

Mary is a better than average cook. She gets surplus commodities, and the chickens, eggs, and garden produce she and J. Harold raise are supplemented by the cheese, peanut butter, rice, canned meat, and other commodities the family draws.

"We get the commodities on the first Thursday of the month," she said. J. Harold puts the smooth, worn bridle on the mule, and rides down to Mills Store, about a mile away, each month to fetch them. J. Harold also helps tend the garden and care for the mule. In the summer he helps pick the blackberries Mary Sizemore cans for the winter meals. "Harold is a good boy and he's got a good education. He completed the eighth grade," Mrs. Sizemore said.

She buys a few groceries. The commodity quota she gets includes flour and lard, enough to last more than half of the month. The canned beef, chicken, and pork in the silvery cans stamped "U.S. Department of Agriculture" are eaten to the last scrap. It costs her fifty cents to get her quota hauled to Mills Store. She has no way to get to Barbourville, nearly twenty miles away, so, like many commodity recipients on Stinking Creek, she pays Hobert Mills the fifty cents to bring the food from the county seat. Hobert Mills takes in the commodity cards, collects the foodstuffs and hauls them up Stinking Creek. It is one of the opportunities available to a man who can afford running a truck on Stinking Creek.

"I went and signed up for welfare oncet," Mrs. Sizemore said. "They said if I didn't get the commodities I could get it. It don't seem right."

Her husband sometimes helps a bit more than the monthly check for $70. "He just drove up not long ago and called some of the young uns down to the road and dropped off some new clothes for them," she said. Mary didn't walk down to the road to see him, but now she was critically examining the new trousers the smaller boys were wearing, gauging the quality and thickness of the deep blue denim between thumb and forefinger.

J. Harold, who had been watching the cops close in on the gangsters in the television movie, sat upright on the bed, kept his eyes on the television screen, and asked his mother casually, "Was that him in that old black Pontiac?"

"That was him," Mrs. Sizemore replied. Harold sank back to watch the gangsters get their grisly justice.

"He won't be back for some time," she said.

Juanita Sizemore was buried two years ago. But the creek was up, the weather was savage, and no proper service with the entire Holiness congregation present was held.

Juanita's heart, weakened by rheumatic fever, finally stopped beating when she was eighteen. For months she had been bedfast, worried over by J. Harold and attended by her mother, and Virginia, her sister. Until one day she saw a vision. Shortly after that she died.

They carried the frail body far up Paint Gap Branch—to the place where the Sizemore dead await the day of Resurrection—and buried it.

Now in the waning days of a hot, airless June, nearly two years later, it was decided to hold a memorial service at the Sizemore burying place for Juanita and any other Sizemores who had not yet had a full church burial.

The Sizemores came, dozens of them, slowly up the steep footpath to the opening where the dead lie in rocky graves, mounded and marked by metal markers driven into the ground at the head of each grave. In the square top of each marker were a name and two dates. One, near the edge of the rows of graves, said "Juanita Sizemore, Born 1945, Died 1963."

At the edge of the clearing, the Sizemores sat on logs, on stumps, and on the ground in the shade of a huge beech tree that thrust aloft immense gnarled limbs, twisted and bent with the years. Against the trunk of the big tree a weathered wooden shelf was nailed. The shelf serves as altar and a resting place for songbooks and a bucket of water with its metal dipper.

This is the "big church," a church in the open, under a tree or under the open sky. Many mountain people will tell you, "I married in the big church." Or, "My daddy and momma were married in the big church." The big church at the Sizemore burying place is a natural amphitheater, sloping gently upward from the huge beech tree. And the Sizemores sat there, watching the others come slowly up the path under a blazing sun, then greeting them as they arrived.

Charles Rourke, a tall man with immense hands, wearing a dark-green shirt and denim trousers, walked to near the front of the big church because he leads the singing. He greeted the bereaved: "Hidy, Mrs. Sizemore."

Service under the big beech tree up on the hill for Juanita Sizemore

Aging, spry Mrs. Easter Sizemore, in a dark flowered cotton dress, fanning herself with a handful of maple leaves, said, "His will be done."

Ed Sizemore, walking stiffly because of his back hurt in the coal mine.

Speed Sizemore edged to a seat near the rear of the big church, poking along with a makeshift cane, a mop handle once painted yellow.

The singing began. The saved ones who had been baptized sat near the front, near the big beech tree. The cousins who come mainly to funerals and weddings sat in a wide semicircle back against the forest wall.

"She's shore got a lot of brothers."

"A lot of hypocrites, you mean."

A suppressed wave of chuckling along the rear rows.

Speed Sizemore moved nearer, smiling broadly in recognition. "I'm still all stove up," he said cheerfully.

The Sizemores—by blood and by marriage—were still finding their way up the hill when Charles Rourke began to lead the singing.

> *"I'm alone in this world . . .*
> *My mother's gone to glory. . . ."*

It was hot and still, as it always is in the high places, shut off from the breeze by encircling walls of beech, oak, poplar, and maple. The rocky graves at the side of the big church thrust their mounds above the encroaching weeds and vines. Goaded by summer heat and driven by the sun and rain, the undergrowth struggles constantly to reclaim the tiny cleared places.

> *"I'm alone in this world.*
> *Take me home, blessed Saviour, take me home. . . ."*

The congregation began to join in the singing gradually, tentatively. Soon there was a full-voiced, vibrant choir: thin high voices wailing; deep voices throbbing; all joining in increasing volume:

> *"I'm a poor wayfaring stranger.*
> *I know dark clouds will gather round me.*
> *I know my way is rough and steep.*
> *I'm going there to join my mother. . . ."*

J. Harold, his face glowing with an unaccustomed scrubbing, sat far to the rear, silently watching. Virginia, her blond-brown hair glinting from a stray ray of sun that stole through the leafy canopy, sat at the very front, singing the hymns by heart.

A mother walked to the tree, gingerly stepping between the worshipers,

filled a yellow plastic baby bottle with water, replaced the dipper in the
bucket, then picked her way back to her brood.

> *"I'm only going over Jordan.*
> *I'm only going home.*
> *I'll soon be free from every trial,*
> *My body asleep in the old churchyard."*

A plump lady arose, her eyes tightly closed, and cried, "I think we
should all give thanks for being alive on this hill this morning." The
congregation rose, and each member held up a hand as the voiced prayers
mingled and echoed across the hill.

Speed Sizemore pointed his yellow-blotched walking stick at a small,
frail man near the front, and announced in a loud whisper: "There sits
the preachin'est man ever was. That's Allen Collitt. They ought to turn
him loose."

It was a service without ritual or format. Led by the saved ones clustered
fervently at the front, the Sizemores sang and prayed as urged individually
by their religious leaders up by the beech tree—even those at the rear,
many of whom rarely attended church. For every Sizemore has loved ones
resting at that spot, and the pangs of loneliness and bereavement were
sharpened by the singing and praying.

A man buried his head in his arms, and wept, his big shoulders jerking
with the agony of his sobs.

A woman touched a grave marker, turned her face skyward, and moaned
hollowly, a long, low cry of despair.

At length Allen Collitt arose. He wore dark slacks and an immaculate
white shirt buttoned tightly at his throat and wrists. He is a small man,
slightly stooped. He is balding in front and his intent eyes peer out from
under the exaggerated domelike effect of his sunburned forehead. His
voice was low and timid, as though reluctant to intrude upon the service.
Almost shyly, he offered to preach "if the loved ones care me to."

A man's voice said flatly, "Go ahead. Preach."

Allen Collitt has mastered the singsong, hypnotic delivery of the mountain preacher. He walked to the base of the beech tree, placed his Bible
on the shelf beside the water bucket, pointed one finger at the assembled
Sizemores, gave his trousers a quick hitch with the other, and preached,
leaping eagerly to his task, so that the perspiration beaded immediately on
his high brown forehead.

"Those who go to sleep in Jesus will arise from this mountain. Jesus
is going to return. Yes, He's coming back." The little preacher threw both

arms aloft in a sweeping gesture. "There'll come a clap of thunder. This mountain will tremble and the rocks will come a-rollin' down. But we're gonna wash our sins in His own blood."

He stepped over to shake the extended hand of a woman who sat on a rock nodding agreement. "I'm just a little preacher, but this morning I feel like a great man in God." He was preaching without prepared text or topic. But he knew the time-tested elements of his religion, and he hurled them at the congregation in a rich scattering of threats and promises:

"Some say, 'Tomorrow I'll make it right.' But tomorrow may never come. May never come for all who raised families and toiled through this life with their bare hands. There's all kinds of evil going on . . . lyin' and cheatin' and hypocrites. God said, 'I hate those things.' "

He preached briefly, passionately, then abruptly took his Bible from the weathered wooden shelf, and sat down.

The saved at the front stood, mingled, and shook hands all around as they sang:

>*"Are you washed in the blood of the lamb?*
>*Lay aside those garments that are stained with sin."*

When every hand was grasped again and again, there were more individual prayers.

Mary Sizemore prayed, her baby fretting on her shoulder: "I thank God for being here. I thank Him for the saved and unsaved both being on this mountain."

Juanita's memorial service was over. Her name had not been mentioned. But she can rest there, her racked body at ease now, until the day the mountain splits open and reveals the great reward to all the Sizemores.

The service in the big church appeared to bring a great peace to Virginia. She spent more and more time sitting silently in the swing on the Sizemore front porch. Virginia was more obsessed with the Lord than she was with boys, so she gazed at the hills and wondered about the hereafter.

Mary Sizemore has tried to raise all her children within the strict concepts of the Holiness Church. J. Harold is still a challenge and a trial for her. But Virginia, Mrs. Sizemore points out proudly, "is saved, praise be."

And Virginia is—wholeheartedly, eagerly, proudly—a vassal of her Maker.

Virginia is a pale, slender girl. Her long legs bear the tiny red marks of well-scratched insect bites, and her long light-brown hair, uncut to comply with the command of the Lord, hangs nearly to her waist or floats in wisps as the winds shift and play in the hollow. Virginia sits in the swing on her front porch, and waits. But she has definite ideas of what she is waiting for.

The swing creaked rhythmically as Virginia nudged the porch floor with her toes. Her pale gray eyes were sincere and trusting. She was wearing a faded pink cotton blouse, a yellow skirt, and yellowish tan leather slippers. A bright red cloth band held her unviolated hair back from her face.

It took courage, but, smiling and wistful, she approached the subject of her religion in a long, circuitous conversation.

"In the Bible it says if you are a real good Christian you are not supposed to cut your hawr and wear this makeup," she said. And in a tone of confession, "Sometimes I wear a little powders."

"You know what I believe?" She pursed her pale lips in concentration, and apparently decided to circle once more before coming directly to what she had on her mind.

"J. Harold likes you," she said. It was a frank compliment. "I think Momma does, too. But that J. Harold. He used to like school 'til he quit. Daddy, when he was living with us, took J. Harold to bad places where Christians are not supposed to go. To the wrestling in Knoxville." She paused, and tears welled in her eyes. "Daddy used to be a pretty good Christian."

Virginia didn't wipe away the tears. She swayed gently back and forth in the swing until the wind dried them.

"Well, I write notes to boys . . . just in school. I don't write no letters and send 'em by mail. Momma won't let me go out with no boys." There was quiet resignation in her voice. "I guess your mother knows what's best for you."

She came back to religion. "We talk to J. Harold about being a Christian, but talkin' just makes him worser. He won't come in the church house hardly. He sits outside there with them old boys.

"Them boys who stay outside the church house, they laugh at you when you shout. Their laughing will turn to tears and cries. The Bible says when the end comes, if you make fun of God and mock him and stuff like that, he will laugh at you and mock at your fears in the end just before you die." Her voice was soft and matter of fact. She leaned back in the swing and smiled knowingly.

It was impossible to lead this wide-eyed child away from the subject of religion. She answered questions quietly, in almost complete detachment.

"I guess you ain't heered the news. We got on the welfare. And we got the commodities. You already knowed that. I guess we'd starved to death

Virginia Sizemore

if it hadn't been for the commodities. Momma knows how to fix them right. So I eat pretty hearty.

"Every once in a while I take a wormy spell. I mix water and turpentine and sugar, and drink that. The sugar makes the worms eat it, and the turpentine makes 'em stop biting on me.

"I'll be in the seventh grade next year. I guess I'll keep on goin'. I'm not old enough to quit. I can't quit nohow on account of Momma's welfare, and I got to go 'til I'm eighteen. Jimmy, he's fifteen, but I caught up with him and passed him." She shook her head in a mild rebuke of her brothers. "Jimmy, he can't learn nothin'. J. Harold can learn, but he's getting out of practice now."

Virginia pushed the long hair back from her thin shoulder and paused to offer a big, deliberate smile. "I was born and raised right here on Stinking Creek," she said. "I been studying about a big city lately. I got a aunt in Louisville. Momma said you got big high buildings there. I been in Knox and Bell County, over the hill thar, and over to Straight Creek."

She was answering the questions patiently, but briefly. She wanted to get back to her religion.

"I like gitar music," she said. "My uncle has a gitar. I can play six chords, but mostly use just four. I'd sure like to get one of them gitars. I can play and sing 'Prayer Bells of Heaven,' 'Beautiful Life,' and 'Old Country Church.' I don't sing none of them jig songs. Momma says I have a right good singin' voice."

Yaller, J. Harold's dog, slumped up on the porch, gave a halfhearted growl for a greeting, and collapsed in the sun. Virginia smiled her big smile again. "I been wantin' to ask you about something," she said.

Here is how she told it, a frail, pale girl alone on a porch high above Stinking Creek, speaking softly and earnestly, her long hair floating and drifting in the afternoon breeze:

"I been dreamin' and thinkin' a lot lately.

"You was to my sister Juanita's funeral. Well, I'm thinkin' about Juanita. When my sister died . . . she was layin' in bed, and the Lord appeared to her with a lamb in His hand. It scared her. She told me and Momma all about it.

"Juanita was eighteen when she died two years ago. She had rheumatic fever for seven years, then took heart dropsy. And she saw this vision.

"I dream about Him some. I dream about girlfriends. Sometimes about Momma and J. Harold. Oncet I dreamed I went in a-swimmin' and some boys were laughin' at me.

"One time I dreamed about the end a-comin'. It was real bright, the sun. Then it turned awful dark . . . the whole world was awful dark.

"I dream about things such as that.

"I joined the church when I was eleven. I was baptized in the creek up by the Thompson place. I felt the power of the Lord on me. Sinner people can't see into how the Lord works. Sometimes He shows you in a dream.

"I had one good friend. We were saved at the same time, but she went back on the Lord. She won't clap her hands and she won't shout in the church house. She sits on the back row with the sinners. I shout a lot. Whenever the Lord moves you, you shout.

"I'll tell you one thing, the power of the Lord sweeps you right off your feet. If you never felt it you don't know what it's like."

She smiled again, a wan but friendly smile, an assurance that what she was about to say was not in criticism.

"You been goin' to the Salem Baptist Church. I heered it. They are good people, but the Baptist don't believe like the Holiness does. They wear this makeup . . . cut their hair. And wearing shorts. Drinkin', I guess. They claim they're Christians.

"Do you understand the Bible? We got a Bible, but it ain't got no back on it. I don't read it too much. I don't understand it too much. The Lord can give a preacher a gift to understand it."

The pale gray eyes were even and fixed. Virginia was calm and relaxed in the squeaking swing, and content with the decision she had made: to reveal how she felt about her religion.

"I don't suppose you believe in handlin' snakes," she said. She didn't wait for an answer. "We believe in handlin' snakes. I believe in handlin' them. I never did handle none, though."

The Holiness Church has long preached a literal belief in the verses from John, James, and Hebrews that call upon believers to take up serpents to demonstrate the power of God to protect His followers. Snake handling, however, was not then being practiced on Stinking Creek, as it was in other parts of the mountains. The practice suffered a severe blow locally when a visiting evangelist from the South took up a copperhead at the climax of a fervent service, was bitten, and died a lingering, painful death.

"God can give you a gift to handle snakes," Virginia was saying. "I wouldn't be afraid if I had the gift. I could if I asked for the gift. I saw them handle a copperhead. They brought this snake in . . . this man got to handling it. Then they'd throw the snake to each other. The way I believe to do it is to go to the box and handle the snake by yourself. I believe when you throw it back and forth, the power of the Lord may leave it.

"That's another thing the Baptist don't believe in. If they don't believe that, they don't believe none of it. If you don't believe the whole word of the Bible, you don't believe none of it.

"I saw them handle serpents when I was about eleven. That's when I got saved."

A fleeting look of concern came to Virginia's face. She cocked her head slightly and there was a frank question on her small features. "I reckon you're saved," she said. "You better do your work in the light, 'cause you can't do it in the dark." And she patiently explained, "Now the light is when you're livin' and the dark is when you're dyin'."

What of the Messer boys and the Mills boys and the Bargos—all the people a scant mile away along the creek, drinking pop and loafing in the store on the bulging bags of cow feed? Of Peggy Mills, wearing shorts and eating a bolgna sandwich? All Baptists. All baptized. And all on treacherous ground according to the Gospel as Virginia Sizemore understood it.

"I pray a lot," Virginia said. "I pray sometimes oncet, sometimes twicet, sometimes three or more times a day. I pray mostly to my ownself for people to get saved and put the devil behind their backs. And I pray to bless each and every one.

"Sinner people don't understand prayin'. I tell you, I never did want to be a sinner person."

The shadows of the scrub sycamores down by the creek were growing longer, and Virginia's mother was banging pots and skillets in the small kitchen. Mrs. Sizemore came out on the porch, and there was a sweetish aroma of cooking blackberries floating out from the kitchen.

Mary Sizemore smiled a tiny smile. "She's been aimin' to tell you about her religion," she said.

There seemed no appropriate goodbye for Virginia. It came out as an attempted friendly, "Maybe you can say a prayer for me someday, Virginia."

The girl nodded. "I was aimin' to," she said.

9 The Young Couples

THERE ARE NOT many young married couples on Stinking Creek. The meek who inherit the earth, in that part of Kentucky, are inclined to take one look at their shabby inheritance, put their children and possessions into an aging automobile, and move to Detroit or Cincinnati or Cleveland or Chicago.

But a few stay. Two of these are Earl Broughton and Truman Messer. They swore they would never leave. But the recent history of Stinking Creek indicates otherwise. The butchered mountains, the polluted creeks, the spirit-killing joblessness, all tend to lead a man down one of two paths: he can become a welfare number or he can try his luck in the city. For the time being, however, Earl Broughton and Truman Messer were determined to live and raise their families on Stinking Creek the hard way—without welfare help.

Up the Middle Fork, past Browns Hollow, to the north and east in a series of lesser hollows, the creek banks are settled by Broughtons. Broughtons took the timber, farmed the narrow bottoms, raised huge generations. Most of them are getting on into their old age, and many of the younger Broughtons are gone to punch time clocks in northern cities.

Earl Broughton has stayed. He is thirty-two, and in twelve years of married life he has accumulated seven children who range in age from one to nine, a reasonably substantial square wooden house, a good wife and a good job. But the job is 240 miles away, in Cincinnati.

Earl is a wiry, energetic man. His hair is red, and the hairs on his strong arms are white, bleached from the sun. He has strength and drive and ambition. So he can, while he is young enough, keep the job in Cincinnati and the home on the Middle Fork of Stinking Creek.

147

He leaves his job in Cincinnati thirty minutes after midnight each Friday and begins to drive his Falcon sedan southward. By five thirty on Saturday morning, if there has been no mechanical trouble, he skids to a halt on the gravel road in front of his house. Then he grabs his seven children, one at a time, pitches them into the air and kisses them as they squeal with their weekly delight. Then, his clothes still on, he drops onto one of the beds in the front room of the four-room house and falls asleep.

He has been working at the plant in Cincinnati since before he got married. He came home to get married. He married Marie Warren, who lived down the creek a mile or so and who was eighteen then.

As long as his strength permits, Earl will keep his job in Cincinnati and his family on Stinking Creek.

"I don't like Cincinnati," he says flatly.

But Cincinnati enables him to feed his family and fulfill his determination to stay off welfare.

"I'm on piecework up there," he said. "I'm a machine operator . . . operate a press. This company makes stove-range hoods, fans, intercoms— things in the building-material line." For operating his press, Earl is paid "an average of about $120 a week, after they take everything out. I pay $13 a week for a room up there, and by the time I eat something, it comes pretty high."

Earl yawned. He was still a bit groggy from his long drive and his brief Saturday-morning nap. He sat on the serviceable overstuffed couch in his living room surrounded by the wife and seven children gathered to enjoy the weekly visit. The room was swept and dusted in honor of the home-coming, and Marie Broughton's busy week was partly evidenced by clusters of freshly ironed children's clothing hung from nails high on the walls.

Marie is a dark-haired woman who at thirty has the quiet competence of the mountain wife. She tried once to move her brood to Cincinnati to keep the family together, but for the Broughtons it can't work out that way.

"I just couldn't handle the kids there," she said. She was sitting on a straight-backed chair leaned against the facing of the open front door. Sunlight poured into her lap, and behind her the hills lay green and serene. "There's no place in a city for the kids," she said. She looked across the room toward her husband, still stretching and yawning on the couch. "No, sir, I don't like it up there. And I don't like to stay away from him, but I got no choice."

Earl beamed a possessive grin. "She likes it wherever I am, I think."

Actually, with the commodity program and the aid to dependent children and other programs, Earl Broughton could sit at home, never work, and be about as well off as he is with his killing schedule. He never seriously considers this alternative.

"N-o-o-o!" It was a definite opinion, long and low and delivered with an arching of his eyebrows over determined blue eyes. "I guess I ain't made for the welfare. I went to the sixth grade, and there was a big family of us . . . eleven of us. We had to do a lot of work together to keep goin'. We did a lot of farming and timbering. And now the timbering is about gone, and the big farms has took over from the little fellows. I'd like to farm. I can't farm on what we got here. Not much bottom around to farm on. But I can work good as any man.

"Sometimes I wonder how the men do it and live with themselves . . . stay on the welfare. I never mention it to none of them. I figure it's none of my business.

"I don't want none of that welfare 'til I can't work, and then I want my share. My daddy never had none of that 'til he had a heart attack and couldn't work, and then it took him almost year to get it. My daddy was sixty-two when he died."

The children were racing into, and then out of, the room to take a playful poke at their father—or to only stand a second and smile. Earl greeted each one with a smile, a friendly slap on the bottom, or a word. He tries to crowd a lot of family life into the brief hours between Saturday morning and Sunday night, when he turns the Falcon sedan back toward Cincinnati.

"We're going to have four in school pretty quick," he said. "You pay their lunch. That's one dollar for each for one week. And give them some spending money and shoes and dresses." But the warmth of his homecoming made it difficult to dwell on the harder facts of life.

He grinned. "I guess we'll have to fight the boys off pretty quick when those girls grow up.

"Now, I ain't totally against the welfare, understand. There'd be lots of them starve if we didn't have it." He was silent for a while. "I hope the government is doing the right thing with this welfare. It takes a few things to build a hollow. There ain't nothing here to start building from 'til we get something to build on. There is just no employment. If there was a factory here, why I'd lay in my application right now."

His wife agreed. "I think they should get some jobs so the men can stay home."

Earl's smile was gone now. "It makes a bad life," he said, "one being in one place and one in another."

Mr. and Mrs. Truman Messer

Truman Messer is a methodical young man, and capable. He has his life planned, and it all revolves around his tiny doll-like house on the bank of Stinking Creek and his pretty wife, Geraldine. They are an attractive, optimistic couple, and they make life seem easy.

Truman is nineteen and Geraldine is seventeen, and they have known each other all their lives. Actually, Truman said, "We only went together steady for one year and three months."

Truman planned his marriage carefully. He has a job in the supply room of the Pineville Community Hospital, about twenty miles away. He works five and a half days a week, and after they have deducted his Blue Cross insurance and taxes, he takes home $125 a month. The Truman Messers think they can get by comfortably on this amount—even if it is less than the checks received by some of the welfare recipients around them.

Truman grew up on the creek, only a few yards from his little house, and has never wanted to live anywhere else.

"When I was little we'd go swimming right here," he said. "Then we'd go to a big mulberry tree and eat mulberries and then go back swimming. Used to fish, too. Used to be plenty of fish in this creek.

"People can make it here if they try," Truman said. Truman and Geraldine were sitting in the neat room that serves as bedroom and living room. There were a blond bed, chest, and dresser, a long turquoise sofa and overstuffed chair, pink table lamps, and scrubbed tan linoleum. There was a television set in the corner by the bed. The room makes up about two thirds of the Messer home. The rest of the little rectangular building houses a neat kitchen filled with bright colors—curtains, oilcloth on the table. The windows let in plenty of light, but the door was closed against the dust from the road.

Truman lounged in a chair, the picture of a young man who has arrived. Geraldine, her bright red hair gleaming, her eyes deepened with blue eye shadow, sat on the arm of the sofa cuddling a large brown Teddy bear.

"He picked out the furniture," Geraldine volunteered.

He did. Methodically, tediously. "I picked it out four months before I got married. It's $700 or $800, and it's all paid off but the TV," he confided. He also papered the bedroom-living room, underpinned the house with stones, and wired the house for electricity. When he brought his bride in, the place was as liveable as it could be made.

Truman Messer is confident. His blue eyes are serene under the thatch of dark brown hair, and his small, compact body is muscular and straight. And his wife is content, something not too commonplace on Stinking Creek.

Hair brushed, face made up, her house clean, she sat dressed in shorts and a tight-fitting blouse, and smiled, cradling the big brown Teddy bear.

"I guess we'll always stay here," Truman went on. "I've not got much desire to move. I got a job once in Detroit when I was on vacation to see how it'd feel. W-h-o-o-e-e!" It was a sound of disgust.

"It was just too crowded. I like it here. The freedom and the hills. Plenty of good fresh air. I think it's a good place to raise a family."

Geraldine Messer giggled faintly. "He's got it planned for two children," she said.

Truman "got in the first six weeks in the first year of high school." Geraldine completed the eighth grade. Most of what they learn now comes from the television set. They feel they can't afford to subscribe to newspapers or magazines.

While Truman is away at work, Geraldine watches the TV and some-times reads. "I read *True Confessions*. Read them since I was ten or eleven," she said. "I read lots of detective books when I can get them. I watch the TV all the time. What I like best is 'The Doctors' and all the dramas."

Truman squirmed in his chair. He thought his young red-haired wife wasn't doing herself justice.

"I give her all the money. People around here don't know how to buy things. She does. She even started a savings account."

"That's right," Geraldine agreed. "People don't budget it right. They don't spend for things they need. They won't buy good food, just knickknacks, pop, ice cream—such as that."

"She's a good cook, too," he prompted. "We got a small garden, and she canned nineteen quarts of beans Monday."

"We don't drink," Geraldine said. "That's expensive around here. And it's illegal."

"Red whiskey costs $2 a half pint," Truman said with some amazement. "We went to church all the time before we were married," he went on. "Now we watch TV, go to the drive-in movie at Barbourville, or just visit our parents. We don't waste much foolin' around."

"It makes him feel better, not on relief," his wife said. "You know you're doing something when you're not drawin' a check."

"I'll tell you this," Truman said. "I think we need some factories and stuff. The mines are all gone and the timber's gone. But I wouldn't work in a mine if there was one. I'd just about try anything before I'd go in a mine or get myself on welfare."

Geraldine squeezed the big brown Teddy bear. "Of course, there is jobs in Detroit and Chicago." Her voice was thin and tentative. "You can do more things . . . more places to go."

Truman shrugged it off. "Next thing I got to do is get this house sheet-rocked," he said. "And I tell you something else. I don't want her to never have to work."

10 Exodus

IT WAS NIGHT IN Chicago, and the breezes that found their way into Uptown from Lake Michigan toyed with the discarded paper and trash. There were few people walking along Sheridan Road, and in the distance there was the occasional roar of the elevated trains. Then a new sound appeared. It was the lusty singing of southern voices, and it came from a converted store building. The words of "Blessed Redeemer" floated on the air, sounding strangely out of place.

The 125-member congregation of the Uptown Baptist Church was holding one of its twice-weekly meetings. Sometimes, during the service, a drunk slumps to the sidewalk outside. The departing congregation steps gingerly around the fallen man without surprise.

"This city is like a nervous cat . . . living in a frenzy," the Reverend George W. Archer, pastor of the Uptown Baptist Church, said. He is a former Kentuckian, and his church is one of the many that Chicagoans call "hillbilly storefront churches."

Uptown Chicago is a hillbilly ghetto. And there are similar slum areas in Cleveland, Cincinnati, Dayton—cities all over the northern Midwest. The ghettos are there because for every Earl Broughton or Truman Messer who clings tenaciously to the sterile soil of his native hollow there are dozens who abandon the hills and go north. The exodus from the Appalachians is the most significant migration of our times. Not since the Okies and Arkies struck out for California thirty years ago have so many desperate Americans gone searching for a place to exist.

Since 1940, 2,000,000 people have picked up their modest belongings and left their hills and hollows. At least 1,200,000 of these left between 1950 and 1960—and 275,000 were from East Kentucky. Between the census of 1950 and that of 1960, the population of Knox County, Kentucky, dropped from 30,409 to 25,258.

154

The Council of the Southern Mountains, which has headquarters in Berea, Kentucky, has long studied the culture, plight, and aspirations of the hillbilly. This agency predicts that of the 8,000,000 people in the nine-state Appalachian area, possibly as many as 4,000,000 will someday join the sickened ranks of the migration.

These are the statistics of despair. Despair for the hillbilly and despair for the police, social workers and municipal agencies that must deal with him in his strange new surroundings. For the mountaineer has become still another paradox. He is white, Protestant, and Anglo-Saxon. Yet his speech, food preferences, music, religion, attitudes toward education and sanitation, and resentment of authority make him a bewildered member of a minority in the country he pioneered.

Dedicated but frustrated, some Northerners who must deal with the hillbilly are beginning to go south to study his origins. One of the better efforts lies in a program the Council of the Southern Mountains conducts at Berea College in Berea.

The campus at Berea is restful and shady, but there were puzzled people walking beneath the ancient oaks and gathered in heated discussions in the brick classroom buildings. These Northerners were there for a serious study of the hillbilly. They had to learn. Their jobs are to deal with the hillbilly on every level—housing, police, welfare, education, employment. These people had never seen a hollow, never visited a mountain store, never attended a mountain church. Now they would. As the days wore on, a few gleams of enlightenment began to appear.

"Hell, I'm beginning to understand why the simple things these people do cause us so much trouble," a husky Chicago police sergeant said. He was puffing and perspiring from a trip up a hollow. "A kid walks up the street to spend a few days with kinfolks while we drag the river. His mother thinks it's okay because they do it here all the time."

The sergeant's reaction is typical, and proof for the thousandth time that though you can read all that is written about the hillbilly, you have to see him to believe him. And among the visiting Northerners, in their classes and over pop in Berea's little drugstore, there was the dawning of an understanding that can be gained only by seeing.

The principal of an elementary school in Columbus, Ohio, said: "I wanted to come see why they migrate. It's very obvious why when you see those ghost towns. My goodness, I wouldn't travel far over these mountains to school either. And I'll be more understanding about cleanliness after seeing how far some people have to walk for water."

A young woman who directs a community center for mountain youth in

Warren County, Ohio, also saw where some of her problems originate. She said: "Their religion is all tied up in it. Teen-age girls won't come to charm school because their parents say it's going against the Bible. They won't let the girls cut their hair or take ballet lessons. They distrust the large established churches and set up 'storefront' churches. I'm dying to attend. The music is terrific. The sound is wonderful. I'd never heard anything like it."

All over the North, transplanted mountain small fry struggle to adapt to strange surroundings.

A teacher at Chicago's Goudy Elementary School, said: "My children take off on Thursdays and later tell me they went home. Home always means Kentucky, no matter how long they've been away. It's not like here. In Chicago they live in tiny apartments with little or no yard. There's no place to play. Their homes are rented by the week instead of the month because they can get together enough money that way. The children don't want to make friends because they're afraid they'll lose them."

An elementary principal from Cincinnati learned something, too. "It's dffficult to be a gracious weekend guest in a home with no toilet."

Some northern schools are rewriting reading material to describe "big apartment buildings and big noises. . . . Kids who lived on Bushy Branch have no conception of little white cottages in neat little villages."

The Northerner who works with mountaineers says he runs into strange silent people whose reactions are unpredictable. They tell of high regard for the pledged work, but a refusal to keep medical appointments. Reluctance to pledge loyalty to unfamiliar creeds causes trouble in labor unions and at church.

Working, sober men cannot understand laws that prohibit them from carrying hunting knives in their own neighborhood. And available jobs for wives and teen-agers tear at the foundations of the traditional mountain patriarchal family structure.

And there are many new fears. A public health nurse in Dayton found that "there's a simple fear of going to the grocery. No wonder. We have those massive supermarkets. In these little stores down here they wait on you."

The language barrier is baffling. A Chicago social worker recalled that "I tried to interview a family, and when I asked, 'Mind if I talk to you awhile?' the man said, 'I don't care.' I thought that he meant 'I don't care to talk,' so I let them go on out."

Many of the workers who study at Berea believe that the physical features of the land are behind many of their problems. "I couldn't comprehend the isolation. You have to travel forever to go two miles."

A social worker from Dayton's Good Samaritan Hospital was wide-eyed when he said, "The isolation . . . it's like a foreign country. I was amazed to see a man walk forty-five minutes just to get over a hill for no apparent purpose. The children are beautiful and bright. But the corruption of the land with strip mines nauseates me. It's amazing that they do it."

In some cities, educators hope to capitalize on the backgrounds of the migrant children and weave them into the local program. An elementary teacher from Dayton said, "The mountain kids teach the city kids about cows and crops. The city kids know all the corners to cut. To them a parent is just somebody to feed them. A mountain kid's whole world is made up of his parents, sisters, and brothers."

The director of pupil personnel in a large city school system says his city has found one way around the problem of communicating with the new youngsters. "We hire a bunch of teachers from Appalachia," he said. His school system had one thousand new children from Kentucky and West Virginia in one year, and one of the better students is assigned to each new arrival "to show them everything from the lockers to the rest rooms. Otherwise, a kid from one of these forty-pupil high schools would be lost."

He also argues that the mountain kid is not a big cause of delinquency. "I studied 770 cases of twelve- to eighteen-year-olds in Juvenile Court. Seventy-six percent came from right there in town. Only 17 percent were born in Appalachia. Many of our local businessmen had expected the figures to be the other way around."

Sometimes the Northerners go back to their labors with new insights and new hopes.

Said a police sergeant from Chicago: "They tell me we've got 511 agencies set up to render some kind of aid, many of them to refer people to the other agencies. We've got to eliminate those agencies that are all mouth and no legs."

Uptown Chicago, an area about sixteen blocks long and ten blocks wide, lies just north of the downtown Loop area and is shut off from Lake Michigan by a narrow strip of lush hotels and apartments. It is "Hillbilly Land" to any Chicagoan, and it gathers in the estimated thirty thousand Southerners who have migrated to the city. In Uptown, a hillbilly is anybody who wears overalls or speaks with a southern accent. In Uptown, a Georgia flatland farmer is a hillbilly.

Half a century ago, the solemn rows of stone and brick apartment buildings looked to a bright future. Their wide marble entrances felt the tread of merchants and professional people. And half a century ago, the Appalachian mountaineers looked forward to a prosperity wrung from the rich coal veins in their mountains. But time and change have brought the two together to face a dismal prospect.

The Southerner tosses his garbage into the alleys as he tossed it into the creeks back home, and looks askance at the tidy Japanese who send their scrubbed children to the same schools with his frequently grubby offspring. He haunts the beer joints on Broadway, Wilson, and Sheridan, and avoids the places where the American Indians gather to drink whiskey and the Puerto Ricans gather to drink wine.

In a bar on Broadway, a Tennessean named Jennings kept his empty beer bottle handy in case of a fight, and muttered, "All a man could rightly want is out of Uptown."

But Chicago offers jobs, the one thing that attracted them all.

Jim Sesco had been there off and on since 1955. When he lived in Pikeville, Kentucky, he worked in the mines. In Chicago, he supports his wife and four children, when he can, with a variety of jobs: gardening, a little painting, and once he operated a drill press. But at the time he was unemployed and drawing $232 a month aid to dependent children.

"I guess I'll stay here," he said. "The old lady wants to stay. But a man can't live on what he gets here." Uptown's cost of living is high. Sesco was paying $74 a month for a dank two-room basement apartment. "And they get $6 for 100 pounds of potatoes here. In Pike County it wouldn't cost a man more than $2 or $3 dollars. Meat doubles itself up here, too."

Sesco has the streak of fatalism found in many mountaineers. "Hard luck runs my way," he said. "My dad got forty-five years in the deep mines, and the day he retired, some slate fell in and broke his back and both legs."

Sesco, at thirty-three, talked like a defeated man. "I aim to look for a job, but a man can't do anything in this town without a car." A lot of the hillbillies don't have cars anymore. Police say they towed in more than four hundred abandoned cars from a square-mile Uptown area within ninety days.

Some never had a car. Wilson Gordon is one of them. "We highwayed it up here from Mississippi," says Mrs. Gordon. "We put four of the kids in foster homes and just put out our thumbs. It was in the wintertime." Mrs. Gordon has seven children. All were with her in Uptown. But Gordon wasn't working.

"I haven't been too well," Gordon explained. "But I could get a job if I could read and write."

In the the daytime, when school is out, swarms of children race through the cluttered alleys and climb the tiers of rear stairways. When asked where they are from, a dozen shrill voices take up an excited roll call of southern states: "Tennessee!" "Alabama!" "Kentucky!"

Then their mothers call them in. Southerners in Uptown don't like strangers. They have been surveyed, questioned, photographed, and analyzed almost daily. A dozen scowling teen-age boys follow strangers down the street, and finally one boys explains: "We've been put on television and made to look like the lowest of the low." Uptown youth are tired of being held up like Chicago's sore thumb for the world to gawk at.

A handful of Uptown children—about 650—were attending the summer program at Stewart Elementary School. It was an "enrichment" program, and included individual help and tours of the city. Stewart, like other schools in Uptown, has a turnover of more than 100 percent each year. Its 1,200 students were born in forty-three states and thirty-three different foreign countries.

A teacher in an "adjustment room" said: "Many parents from Appalachia appear extremely interested in getting an education for their children. They all want to know, 'Is my child normal?' "

Asked if she had any children from Appalachia, a teacher replied, "Look and see if you can pick them out yourself." You can. They are fair-complexioned, and usually dirty and shy.

One little girl said she was from "Pine Creek."

"Where is that?"

"I don't know."

"Is it in the mountains?"

"I think so."

The teacher shrugged. "Their homes aren't conducive to education."

Their homes are tiny apartments partitioned off in the big buildings. The years have changed the original colors of the walls, carpets and drapes into depressing grays and browns. Sometimes several families share a bath or a kitchen.

One landlady says she gets "no trouble from the hillbillies. Only trouble I had was a veteran, with a steel plate in his head, got drunk and threw all the fire extinguishers down the stairs."

Another landlady said flatly, "I don't want any hillbillies in my place." She leaned against the rotting doorway of her own apartment, and added: "What they want is a public playground. Nobody knows how much stuff I've gotten broke around here. Those people must be deaf and dumb. I ask how come a window got broke, and nobody knows anything. I'd make more money if I tore it down and made a parking lot than I would renting to hillbillies."

As night falls, Uptown changes. Children disappear from the streets, and the alleys are silent. The blare of the jukeboxes increases, and the bright blue-and-white patrol cars of the Chicago police multiply. Only the incessant roar of the elevated trains remains unchanged. The police break up groups wherever they gather to talk, but nobody bothers the girls who solicit in the bluish light of the neon sign atop the nondenomenational North Shore Church. The sign proclaims: "Christ Died for Our Sins."

A cabdriver said philosophically, "The hillbillies work hard and they drink hard. They make it rough for everybody." He said that the Southerners stick to their own beer joints and are rarely seen in the striptease joints. "They usually only beat each other up," he added cheerfully.

A man behind a counter of a small café pulled up his T-shirt, revealing a long scar across his chest. "A hillbilly done that," he said.

Many men roam Uptown after dark. Most appear aimless. One who roamed with a purpose was the Reverend George Morey of the United Presbyterian Church. A minister-at-large, he tried to do what he could for the migrants' spiritual well-being. But he was a little shaken. "I was solicited by three fourteen-year-old girls," he said. He watched a Southerner choke his common-law wife in front of a bar. "We have a long way to go here," was Mr. Morey's understatement, and he offered a bit of advice: "Don't go in Kelly's bar. It's very rough."

In Kelly's, the jukebox blared Hank Williams' "Your Cheatin' Heart," but a cooling breeze was moving in from the lake, and tempers were not high that night.

Others are willing to help on the long road back to respectability. Stocky, jovial John Kawash, the Republican precinct captain, steers Southerners to appropriate agencies, and rounds up cigar boxes and materials for youngsters to use in projects at the local office of the Council of the Southern Mountains. The Uptown office of this Berea-based organization is doing what it can. In a back room, an aide helped a nineteen-year-old girl learn her ABC's. And a volunteer college coed worker smiled encouragement as a woman, apparently in her sixties, read from flash cards: "Cow. Dog. Lion."

The McCormack Boys' Club, one of the biggest in the country, struggles for the future of Uptown boys. It has 3,050 members who pay $1 a year. The club's $1.5 million building houses a professionally staffed dental clinic, eye clinic, an optometrist, swimming pool, and gym. It can do anything for a boy from providing a haircut to administering a battery of personality and aptitude test.

"More than half of our boys are from the South," Errol Sewell, assistant director of the club, said. "In fact our all-star basketball team was made up of southern boys."

Sewell added: "The southern boys have a lot of pride. They just don't complain. But they talk a lot about going back home. You pick up an undertone of their great want of attention and affection."

Another who was trying to help was Republican Alderman Robert O. O'Rourke, whose Forty-eighth Ward includes Uptown. "The Southerner is judged by what a few do," O'Rourke said. "He is extremely difficult to reach." He said that other groups—Japanese, Negro, Puetro Rican—are met by the churches when they move into Uptown and have strong social and political organizations. "The Southerner is victimized something awful," O'Rourke said, "by credit he can't afford and by garnishments. He is not at all interested in politics, and he won't vote. That's an unfortunate situation." O'Rourke says the storefront churches might reach the Southerner, but the hillbilly has a deep distrust of the large organized churches. "Down South, the church is very social," O'Rourke said. "Up here, it usually isn't."

Police Captain John T. Fahey, commander of the Nineteenth District in the Uptown areas, also said a few Southerners give all a bad name. "Some of them, instead of going home and sleeping it off, fight it off." Fahey said. "People figure all the hillbillies are like that." Fahey said the Southerners have no leaders, unlike other groups in Uptown. And he adds, "Half the people they call hillbillies come from right here in rural Illinois or Indiana."

Southerners commit no more crimes, except perhaps assault, than do others in this district, Fahey finds. A policeman for thirty-one years, he said he learns something new from the mountaineers every day.

"Their ideas on wife beating. I tried to talk to a man, and told him: 'Look, you've got four kids. What if they found out you beat up their mother? Why did you do it?'

"The hillbilly said, 'She got out of line and I stomped her.'

"I said, 'What would you have done if your father had done it to your mother?'

"The hillbilly said, 'He did it all the time.' "

Fahey said that as soon as the Southerner can afford it, he moves out to the suburbs and forgets all about Uptown. "He never has anything to do with the others again."

A surprising number make it to the suburbs, despite the troubles caused by the ones who are on relief, on the bottle, or too deep in despair. Jimmy Dotson may be one of the few to make it. He talked over a cup of coffee in a small place beneath the elevated train tracks just off Wilson Street, the mainstream of Uptown. Jimmy cradled his cup in two strong calloused hands and talked of his hopes:

"A man takes a lot if he wants to stay out of trouble up here. I only had one fight so far." His flat, twanging mountain voice sounded strange and out of place, almost lost in the metallic rumbling of the elevated trains and the bubbling accents of the Japanese, the Puerto Ricans, and an occasional American Indian.

Jimmy was twenty-seven, and had come reluctantly to Chicago's Uptown only a few months before from Pike County, Kentucky, after the bulldozer and the coal auger replaced him in the coalfields. Jimmy was earning $1.75 an hour operating a molding machine. He was trying to learn to live with the elevated trains and the complexities and the crowding of the city—and without a creek to swim and fish in.

"My wife and me go bowling and to the restaurants around here," he said. "And I stay out of bars. Drinking and stuff like that is just trouble. Somebody always wises off at you."

The Dotsons had a four-room apartment. They had no children, and the four rooms were a real luxury for Uptown. They cost Jimmy $28.50 a week.

Dotson twirled his empty cup in his capable hands and shrugged off the offer of more coffee. His voice was almost swallowed up in the thunder from the elevated tracks:

"I'll probably never go back to Pike County. A man can make it up here, if he really tries . . . I think."

11 The Do-Gooders

NO AREA SUCH as Appalachia could long escape gleeful discovery by do-gooders, those fervent, tireless Americans among us who are driven, as though by demons, to do unto others. So for decades, Appalachia has been done unto. The desolate hollows have swallowed up legions of pious, prim, pathetic little men and women who have braved the wilderness to spread the light. The aching mountains have felt the purposeful tread of zealous social reformers. Missions representing almost every denomination and sect have unfurled their banners of brotherhood in hollow after hollow. Appalachia is Mecca for those driven—both by demons and by self-guilt—to do unto somebody, somehow.

But among the sinners there have been saints. There have been selfless, dedicated, and skilled people who have willingly and literally sacrificed themselves to bring a glimpse of hope to tiny blessed areas here and there in the vast wasteland of defeat that is Appalachia.

Two women live in a boxy, two-story old frame house at the mouth of Kenningham Branch. They are known all up and down Stinking Creek and its tributaries as "the dark-haired nurse and the light-haired teacher." The two came there to serve the people of Stinking Creek and it is well known that when one or the other is needed, day or night, in any emergency, from harvesting a crop to delivering a baby, they will "come at a hard lope." The women are Peggy Kemner and Irma Gall, and the big house, with its surrounding acreage, is appropriately named "Lend A Hand."

Peggy, the nurse, was thirty-five. She had dark-brown hair, cropped rather short, shy dark eyes, and small, femininely capable hands. She grew up in Pennsylvania, a member of the Church of the Nazarene. After Eastern Nazarene College, near Boston, Peggy took nursing training at Johns Hopkins and emerged a registered nurse. Midwifery interested her, and she did

Irma Gall, left, and Peggy Kemner

a term paper once on the Frontier Nursing Service, a group of horse- and jeep-borne women who deliver the babies and attend the sick in a mountain section of Kentucky. In September of 1955 Peggy came to Kentucky, a young, determined frontier nurse herself.

At about the same time that fall, another girl from the North came into the Kentucky hills. This was Irma, who was thirty-three. Like Peggy in dedication, she was unlike her in other ways. Irma is gregarious, outgoing; Peggy, quiet and reserved. Irma was a farm girl, and her light-brown hair and strong hands are tinted by summer suns and winter winds. She grew up on a farm in Indiana and she has a deep love and understanding of the soil. She is a devout member of the Church of the Brethren and when she graduated from Manchester College in 1955, she hoped to realize a years-long ambition to move to New Mexico and work among the Indians. She had the qualifications—she was strong, willing, and her frank gray eyes knew no fear.

Irma's church had a mission at Flat Creek, Kentucky, and that is where Irma was persuaded to go, giving up her dream of living among the western Indians. The church ran a one-room school at Flat Lick; and when the new teacher from Indiana showed up, the neighbors estimated her tenure at not more than two weeks. She was their fifth teacher, then a fresh twenty-three-year-old girl who looked more like eighteen. Four previous teachers had been sent packing. Irma appeared to be an easy fifth conquest. But the two dozen students looked into Irma's firm gray eyes, listened to the ring of sincerity in the low voice, and Irma stayed.

Irma improvised a curriculum as best she could. "We took hikes, talked, had a few cookouts. I started a Sunday school in a little building below the school," she recalled.

It was inevitable that the two—Peggy the nurse and Irma the teacher—should meet. They did, and became friends that fall, and they struck upon an idea. "One day I was doing my record books, and I turned to Peggy and asked, 'Why don't we combine and have a self-supporting mission, sort of?' " Peggy was eager. She had developed a desire to serve the mountaineers she now knew and liked, by becoming a midwife. Kentucky is one of the few states that sanctions midwifery.

The new project created new and bigger problems for the two girls, who rode the hills on horseback, looking for a place to serve. There had to be money; there had to be a doctor available "to back Peggy"; there had to be a teaching job for Irma; and there had to be a place.

By August of 1958, the two girls were ready. They had canned food and raised all the money they could—a starting nest egg of $1,000. Much of it was earned by Irma, who went back to Indiana and hired herself out as a painter of farm buildings.

The search for the "the place" began. The two girls rode through hollow after hollow, and one day they gazed up a narrow valley where Kenningham Branch winds down toward Stinking Creek. "This is it," the two girls said simultaneously. They were looking down upon an ancient empty frame building. Weeds grew to the roof, and a corn crop had been planted up to the windows on one side. Behind the house, a neglected barn sagged and creaked with the fall winds. Another small structure stood on the creek bank, a long-deserted store building, a small wooden room with iron bars still across the two front windows. It represented a long-forgotten and unwise investment in the commercial future of Kenningham Branch.

The two girls crossed the creek and approached the vacant, defiant windows of the big house, picking their way between the weeds and stones. The untended hollow was what was left of land deeded long ago to a Colonel George Patterson. He was given the hollow by the government in pay for his services during the Revolutionary War. Colonel Patterson was buried in the garden plot beside the house, which was known to be "hainted." But it was a moment of excitement for Peggy Kemner and Irma Gall.

The two girls stared at the house briefly; then Irma fished a skeleton key from her pocket and turned the rusty, stubborn lock on the door. Inside, the house was equally uncared for. "The walls were black, and there were two inches of silt on the floor—a regular sandpile from the last flood," Peggy recalled.

Irma waded the creek to look for a neighbor. The first woman she met told her that the old "hainted" house had been deluged with twenty-eight feet of water during the most recent flood. Kenningham Branch, like all creeks, does flood, but the figure was an obvious exaggeration. Similar discouraging stories were repeated wherever the two girls checked. The truth was, they said, "Nobody wanted us to move in."

But the place belonged to Ed Kenningham, a taciturn mountaineer who listened to the strange outsiders with some bewilderment, scratched his head, and eventually said: "Girls, I can't rent it. It ain't fit to live in." But he politely listened to their pleas, and finally agreed, "If you girls want to fix it up, well, that'll be rent enough."

For a while, Peggy and Irma stayed on Stony Fork in the adjoining county and rode over every day to work on the old house. The challenge was there. Paint had long since disappeared from the bleak walls. On the floor were seven layers of linoleum, with alternate layers of mud. It was eventually left that way. "We figured it would keep the kitchen warm," Peggy said. The collapsing barn was replaced with one made from rough lumber. The old store was cleaned out and made into a tiny chapel.

Just as the neighbors were reluctant to admit the two, the local school officials were reluctant to hire Irma. "I had to have a job or the whole thing would be lost," she said.

She finally got her job. Alex School is perhaps the most inacessible school in Knox County. A one-room shack, it sits far up a hollow and for much of the way the rocky, bumpy bed of Alex Creek is the roadway. This is the school Irma got, and her $3,000 yearly salary meant financial salvation for the new mission. From the old house to the school, the distance was eight miles, and Irma went to her chores on horseback. "The horse was quite an attention-getter," she said. The two got attention, but little or no help.

Peggy also was visiting the hollows on horseback, and when the word spread that she was a nurse the mountain people felt a new interest in the two girls. When illness and pain strike in the more remote hollows, there often is no way to reach a doctor in town. Peggy's first patient came in October, and the nurse began her career on Stinking Creek in a room of the old house that was converted into a clinic. The equipment consisted of an examining table made from used oak boards and a small satchel of equipment and medicine. Today, the clinic is little more, but it has served hundreds of the mountain people. Peggy has delivered more than two hundred babies, most of them in tiny mountain homes without running water, heat, or light.

During floods, the sturdy examining table plays a dual role. "We put our stuff on it. We got four inches of water in the house two years ago," Peggy said.

Peggy's professional life is a busy one. Worms and malnutrition are the most frequent complaints of her patients. She passes out vitamins, treats colds and diarrhea, and attends to the many small injuries and broken bones that befall the mountaineer and his children. The patients who used to ring the rusty cowbell outside the clinic door and demand penicillin have learned that Peggy can be adamant. "They know now that there are things I won't do without a doctor's order," she said.

Early in the life of their project, Peggy and Irma made two decisions. They named the old house "Lend A Hand," and they agreed not to become an agency for passing out money, free food and clothing, or free service, on the theory that greater respect would be obtained if the patients paid something. So medicines were sold at cost, and Peggy's fee for delivering a baby on Stinking Creek is $25—and this includes prenatal and postnatal care.

About two thirds of the people Peggy cares for pay their bills. But some don't, and a few of these own cars, and their unpaid-for babies watch new television sets.

Peggy, the nurse, screens her patients to prevent disasters. Although many a mountaineer is perfectly willing to turn over a badly hemorrhaging wife to the "dark-headed nurse," such cases often belong in a hospital, and Peggy usually wins the argument.

When asked why malnutrition and worms still persist in an area where welfare checks now sprout like crabgrass, Peggy's answer was direct:

"Worms are difficult to get rid of. The kids play in dirt and are reinfected constantly. I think a lot of the malnutrition comes because the kids get too much pop and candy. If you don't eat things like tomatoes, you don't get Vitamin C." As simple as that.

Peggy was still delivering babies at the rate of two or three a month, but admitted, "I'm interested in planned parenthood, so I guess I'm defeating my own purpose in a way."

People along the hollows, their tiny houses crammed with children, are interested in birth control. But birth-control devices require some cooperation, a commodity not readily available. Peggy encourages the use of vaginal foam and vaginal tablets, and sometimes the program is successful. Sometimes there are only excuses: "Well, I been meanin' to try it."

Peggy has heard plenty of excuses. The horse was eventually replaced by a jeep, which was eventually replaced by an agile International Harvester Scout, which Peggy now uses to climb the hills and cross the streams. She took up her little black bag of instruments, climbed into the Scout one day, and announced she was going to visit "her babies."

To watch Peggy attack the mountain roads in the little green vehicle is answer enough for critics of women drivers. Her route followed the long, climbing crease in the mountain chain along which Roaring Fork flows. In and out of the creek bed, over rocks and through monstrous ruts and gullies, Peggy serenely charged, the four-wheel-drive vehicle clawing for traction. On such a ride two things keep one occupied: breathtaking scenery and preventing your head from crashing out through the metal top.

At the top of the hollow, in a lonely log cabin, a sick baby boy waited, whimpering on an unkempt bed. His uncommunicative mother sat nearby. Peggy made a sling from a diaper, placed the baby in it, and suspended it from a small scale. When the baby was weighed, wiped, and checked, some medicine was left for the sad-eyed mother to administer.

Then back down the creek, past occasional mountainside homes sheltering

*Peggy Kemner teaching
Sunday school in the
converted store building at
Lend A Hand*

*Peggy Kemner, standing,
and four of "her babies"
she delivered*

flocks of children, many of whom are "Peggy's babies." Houses filled with
shrill cries from the youngsters and excuses from the older people.

"Are you practicing birth control? Can the children come down to
Lend A Hand for Bible lessons?"

"We been aimin' to."

"We got beans needs pickin'."

"Them berries got to be picked right now."

"I'll study on it, Miss Peggy."

Peggy reasoned and argued. At length she turned the Scout back into
the creek bed on the homeward journey. "I get a lot of miscarriages," she
said. "They get out to a phone and call me. I try to tell them that if she's
hemorrhaging that much, she has to go to a hospital. But they say, 'No,
I want you to see her first.' Often she can bleed to death. I have to get her
in the Scout and haul her out to where you can get a car in."

While most of the Stinking Creek folk are willing to benefit from the
minor miracles performed by Peggy, they are reluctant even to observe
the minor miracles that have occured down at Lend A Hand itself. Peggy
and Irma soon bought ninety acres, part of it bottom land, which stretches
out from the junction of Kenningham Branch and Stinking Creek. What they
have done with farm practices could be a boon to others in the hollows.
But few come to see.

Doing the work themselves, with tractor and mule, they have demon-
strated ways to plant, fertilize, and spray corn, and have been experiment-
ing with different kinds for livestock feed. The characteristics of different
pasture grasses and hay have been proved. They raise beets for feed. The
sturdy barn they built is filled. The barn itself is stained and preserved with
a coating of used motor oil. Cows, chickens, domesticated rabbits, pigs, and
the mule contribute to the betterment of Lend A Hand.

Recently, the two girls bought another five hundred acres that extend
up the hollow, and have begun a tree planting program. They had set out
more than eighteen thousand pine seedlings, a cover badly needed on many
of the hills to help control soil erosion and check floodwaters.

The original house, which had seemed so desirable to the two eager
girls seven years before, was sagging in the death posture of doomed
houses. A new Lend A Hand was being built, higher on the hill and out
of reach of Kenningham Branch when the spring and fall tides sweep the
valley. Few things interrupt the labor. One rare pause came when Irma
broke her leg while dragging logs from the mountainside with her tractor.

The vegetable garden, which surrounds old Colonel Patterson's grave, is
another experiment. Heavy paper fertilizer bags were sewn together and

laid over the plowed garden spot. Holes were cut in the paper and the seeds pushed down through these, into the ground. The plants grow up through the paper covering, which keeps down weeds. The yield—tomatoes, strawberries, corn, squash, pumpkins, beans, sweet potatoes, and other vegetables—has been increased by a third, Irma said. And there are other advantages. The covering retains moisture in the soil during dry periods. Immediately after a rain, you can walk out into the garden upon the covering without sinking into mud. Irma said another unforeseen benefit developed: the ground stays loose so she can actually reach into the soil, "feel the potatoes, and leave the little ones to grow more."

Ways to coax more bounty from the soil are constantly being sought at Lend A Hand. But not many people appear interested.

Other miracles—for Stinking Creek—occur in the old house's big kitchen. On a rainy summer Saturday morning the kitchen fills with a cloud of heady aromas. Apple pies, blueberry loaf, good things from the hills and hollow suddenly seemed to be plentiful, being prepared for the two big freezers at Lend A Hand. The kitchen has a yeasty, delicious smell, the classic odor of the country kitchen. And nearly everything came from the land around it. Peggy and Irma organized a 4-H Club and are attempting to show youngsters how to cope with their environment. The Lend A Hand club is a consistent winner at local fairs in canning, dressmaking, cooking, livestock raising—rare skills in this rural paradox.

Perhaps some of the younger people will someday benefit from the lessons they learn at the 4-H Club at Lend A Hand. They are shown how to break away from the ritualistic diet of grease and blandness. A very good Spanish rice can be made from the rice and meat that come in the drab commodity packages and tomatoes from the garden. The commodity beef and kidney beans can be made into chili soup. Baking is another field for exploration. In Kentucky, they make what has been known as "the Kentucky cake," a heavy, soggy chunk. And, Irma said, "They look at biscuits as an uninspiring staple. Biscuits can be an art."

That rainy Saturday morning in the big kitchen at Lend A Hand was one of those rare days when no outside problems intruded. The big summer drops splashed on the paper-covered garden outside the window and into the flowing water of Kenningham Branch, which swept by behind a long earth dike Peggy and Irma have thrown up with their tractor to protect the house from flooding. There were no babies to be delivered, no patients to shatter the peace with the rusty cowbell hanging outside the clinic door, and nothing to be done in the fields.

"Brunch," they called it. At nine thirty they went into the dining room and gathered around the big table made from a door. Somehow, the occasion had a festive air, an unexpected and welcome moment of leisurely conversation. Peggy served the brunch: toasted cheese sandwiches made from commodity cheese a friend had given them, peanut butter and crackers, instant coffee, and bowls of the still-warm blueberry loaf. There were two others at the table, two children who laughed and smiled and appeared to be perfectly at home—which, it developed, they were.

Judy Warren was 17, a slender, graceful mountain girl with brown hair and blue eyes. Her brother, Andy, was twelve. Andy has the hard-to-control energy of a rapidly maturing boy accustomed to the out of doors, and he feels more at home riding the mule or fashioning a slingshot from a forked tree branch than he did at table. But he was quiet and scrubbed and ravenous.

The Warren children are two acquisitions of Lend A Hand that result from a permanent policy there. Whenever children encounter unusual hardship, are abandoned, or live too far up a hollow to get out daily to school, there usually is a place for them at Lend A Hand. Judy and Andy had been there since their mother died fifteen months earlier. Their father, long before that, had wandered elsewhere, as many East Kentucky fathers do. Even before their mother died, Judy had lived at the center "off and on" so that her high school education would not be interrupted. The Warrens lived far up Roaring Fork, and Judy was not physically equal to the long hike up and down the creek during floods or in freezing weather.

The prayer Peggy offered as grace at that midmorning meal was appropriate. She said, "Let's ask Jesus to forgive us all and be kind to all who need us."

Religion is a common ground on Stinking Creek. It is possible to find people who are only mildly interested at a particular moment in politics, welfare, baseball, or crops. But religion is a subject all are interested in, and it alone opens all the doors. So where Peggy and Irma have often drawn only blank stares and excuses with birth-control programs, crop betterment, reforestation, and other such endeavors, their weekly Sunday-school classes are an established success.

The old store building beside the big house has become chapel and Sunday school for dozens of Stinking Creek children. Each Sunday morning Peggy and Irma make the rounds of the hollows in the Scout and a Ford station wagon and bring in the pupils. They gather in the converted store building.

The chapel is a small, rectangular wooden building made of rough lumber. The iron bars still nailed to the inside of the front windows are the only remaining evidence of the role the building was intended to play. Huge wooden double doors open from the front and are left open to admit the breeze on warm Sunday mornings. In the center of the door, a polished wooden cross is suspended on a string. The cross revolves slowly in the breeze, turning first to one side, then the other. Inside, the wide vertical boards of the walls are decorated with large brightly colored biblical scenes. There are Jesus healing the sick and Jesus preaching at the Sea of Galilee. Across the rear, bookcases are filled with books, including Bibles and hymnals, which add their own musty smell to the faint aroma of the aging wood. An old pew stretches across the rear, and in front of it are rows of steel folding chairs. There is a wooden podium at the front and an upright piano stands against the wall to one side.

There were twenty-five children in the room, squirming eagerly on the hard chairs. Irma was at the podium. Here is where Irma and Peggy try to equate for the youngsters the strange-sounding words in the Bible with everyday life on Stinking Creek.

There is a gay, joyous, lilting air to the Sunday school, quite unlike the fatalistic approach elsewhere. The children sang "Take Time to Be Holy," and when the last thin echo had died, Irma asked:

"What does that verse say? When things are rushing around us, we will become like Jesus only if we talk and speak like Him." Tiny brows knit in an attempt to understand as Irma, the teacher, smiling and assuring, promised, "If you want to become like Jesus, you have to spend a lot of time with Him. We practice living here on earth so we will know how to live when we get to heaven."

And Irma, the teacher, gently admonished the intent young audience, "Are you all clean enough to be with God? If you are clean in God's sight, then God says, 'I need you. I need you to go home and be a guiding light.' " Most of the children smiled understanding.

Then they sang the rhythmical children's hymn, "Jesus Wants Me for a Sunbeam." It was all hope and gladness, and no brimstone.

After this assembly, the children were divided into classes according to age: Peggy with a group in the dining room discussing the burning bush; elderly, gentle Mrs. Kenningham in the living room with the smallest ones, their hesitant fingers gripping crayons and coloring pictures of a little girl helping an old lady; Irma in the chapel asking, "How much better would Stinking Creek be if parents offered something each morning to God?"

Irma has a knack of asking questions that suddenly make it seem perfectly logical that Stinking Creek is important in the divine scheme of things. Some of her young charges nodded a wide-eyed affirmative, when she asked, "Do you ever see any signs of the Devil walking around on Stinking Creek?"

Irma and Peggy are no less observing of the adult mind on Stinking Creek. They see and feel and understand many of the complex traits that make up the mountain psyche. They are not among the zealous workers who prattle of lost lambs and a goody-goody, senseless evangelism.

Sometimes the two girls take direct action to make a point, as when they once shared a field of corn with a Stinking Creek citizen who refused to pay his share of the cost of fertilizer. The solution was typically simple. "We planted eight rows with fertilizer, then eight without fertilizer, and so on. We harvested the fertilized rows."

And they analyzed the people they are dedicated to helping:

"We are insecure in our children's love around here. Fathers and mothers don't love. The child grows up insecure. There is only a strong sense of tradition. They often don't know love.

"The best thing for this part of the country would be something to give people a sense of dignity and a meaning to life." A tall order, but Irma said it could be done. She sees three steps to take toward this goal:

"First, a job, an income that they can be proud to earn.

"Second, a sense of sensitivity in the home . . . pride in the home and the environment around them.

"Third, a real reason to live . . . security in what they are living for . . . a rediscovering of why they are living."

The strange type of selfishness, practiced with something approaching dignity, puzzles all careful observers. Children are often left to raise themselves; then, as the parents grow old, there is an effort to bring the children back to care for them. A man will fight for a friend, then charge him fifty cents to run an errand.

"A lot of these people like to shout on Sunday," Irma said. "That's perfectly all right—if they live up to the shouting all week."

Many of the children on Stinking Creek were being raised to shout. Some were not, and one of these was Judy Warren, who was being raised by Peggy and Irma.

Judy Warren, her mother dead and her father gone, had at seventeen endured her share of heartbreak. But now, with the rare care and understanding she finds in the big house at Lend A Hand, she is maturing quietly and wholesomely. She has books and some intellectual curiosity around her. And even though she missed many days of school when she lived in the little house far up Roaring Fork, her high school grades are now average.

Judy Warren

She is recovering from the missed classes and the inadequacies of the one-room school she did attend when she could.

Judy is candid, and wise beyond her years in an ability to see people for what they are. On a sunny afternoon she sat on the long back porch at Lend A Hand and talked about her hopes.

"Well, I'm sort of a castoff," she said. "I get homesick for Momma."

The first time Judy moved into the big house on Kenningham Branch was when she was in the fifth grade and had appendicitis. For a long time she was unable to walk back and forth up the long hollow. So she was moved in with Irma and Peggy. "I could stay other places," Judy said, but her voice was suddenly unconvincing. And in a few moments she added, ". . . but I'd have to pay rent or something. I didn't have any money. If I had to have a big favor . . . well, I don't know about the people around here.

"I'm not serious about boys now. I wish I could go to college. Home Ec, that's what I'd like to take. I like sewing best." It is one subject in which she has considerable skill. She later won the dress revue championship at the county fair.

She worried about her future. "I'll have to get a job somewhere sometimes. I may go to Chicago and see my uncle. He lives in Uptown."

Judy, like most teen-agers on Stinking Creek, was curious about the unfamiliar young people who were beginning to appear in the hollows. These newcomers were advance troops in something called the "War on Poverty," and they concerned themselves with everything from painting schools to organizing horseshoe-pitching contests. They were something comparatively new in the hollows, and they were watched with interest—and sometimes met with cooperation—by the mountain people.

Judy is one of the few who discussed them candidly. "Some are nice," she said. "And some are snobby. They have the idea they want to come here and do something, but it's not like they think. Some of the things they say are cutting; because I live here, it's like making fun of me. Some of them say the expressions around here are silly; and they say them over and over, and laugh.

"The people who came in here now—well, their standards of living are different and they don't understand at first. They don't have outhouses and things like that."

The strange new people Judy encountered in the hollow were the advance wave of a bold attack upon Judy's way of life. When they have finished their work, there may be no outhouses on Stinking Creek because there will

be no place for outhouses in the Great Society. There also will be no place
for polluted streams, abused mountains, ugliness, hunger, suffering—or
poverty. The Great Society has been solemnly pledged by Washington, and
the timetable for its accomplishment is somewhat more urgent than that
of the Resurrection, which is generally conceded to be an event of the
somewhat distant future. The Great Society also appears to be better financed. And while it may not entirely replace the Resurrection as the
ultimate hope of the hillbilly, it should make the waiting more comfortable.

As Judy sat on the back porch of Lend A Hand and worried about her
future, she was not completely aware that the United States was involved
in two wars. One was against the Viet Cong in Vietnam, and the other, the
War on Poverty, was being waged within our own borders. Each war has
had its casualties, its heroes, its patriots, and its detractors. Each was under-
going a change called "escalation." The way to escalate a war is to do what
you have been doing on a grander scale. The weapons in Vietnam are
guns and planes and soldiers. The weapons in the War on Poverty are
dollars. But guns and men arrive at no permanent solutions in war, and
dollars alone cannot eradicate poverty.

The troops in the War on Poverty are largely dedicated, but sometimes,
like their co-patriots in Vietnam, they find themselves struggling on strange
ground among a strange people.

The established welfare quagmire in this nation already absorbs more
than twenty billion dollars a year—perhaps thirty billion. The new beach-
head being established on poverty by the Office of Economic Opportunity
was the beginning of an assault at an initial cost of one billion dollars a
year.

Our government estimates there are thirty-five million poor Americans.
If these unfortunates were polled, they would probably estimate that there
are an equal number of Americans dedicated to elevating them to affluence.
In addition to the Office of Economic Opportunity, there are rank upon
rank of agencies born to serve the poor. Of more recent vintage, the Appalachian road-building venture will pour millions into that area; there are
training classes under the Manpower Development and Training Act; there
are programs in the Agriculture Department, the Health, Education, and
Welfare Department; there are programs with almost every conceivable
alignment of federal, state, and local collusion.

But the glamor program now was the Office of Economic Opportunity's
widely publicized array of Job Corps camps, Head Start, Vista Volunteers,
Neighborhood Youth Corps, Community Action Programs, and others. The
OEO has tied controversial strings to the money it sends to fight poverty.

It asks that the poor themselves be permitted to have a voice in their own uplift, and it attempts to prevent local political hierarchies from using the money to perpetuate their own power. Local communities prefer money without strings, except, of course, the traditional patronage lifelines. But strings or not, the money is accepted. Many of the dollars are finding their way into Knox County, which has been selected as a "pilot" battleground in the war.

The way to get federal money to combat poverty is to know how to ask for it. If, for example, the Congress should vote vast funds for "community enrichment and recreational development to combat cultural isolation," it would be of little avail to drop a postcard to Washington and request a "chunk of dough to get some horseshoe games going."

If, on the other hand, the request were a neatly typed presentation—with stacks of carbon copies—for funds to institute "community enrichment and recreational, etc. . . . ," then there would be knowing smiles in the busy offices at the Capital. Forthwith, a "chunk of dough" would be dispatched, and before you could say "cultural disenfranchisement" the thud of pitched horseshoes would resound throughout the hollows.

To this end, Knox County, early in the skirmishing against poverty, organized a Knox County Economic Opportunity Council, Inc., made up largely of local cultural and business leaders. This agency administers the largess distributed by the Office of Economic Opportunity.

A few weeks before the courthouse was dedicated, this county council brought to town, at a salary of $12,000 a year, the man who was to be its chief community planner against poverty. He is James Kendrick, a young man of disquieting intelligence whose visions were at sharp variance with the established pace of betterment in Knox County. He was considered with some awe by the Republican fathers of Knox County because James Kendrick knows exactly how to prepare the proposals—complete with carbon copies—which loose huge funds from the bulging coffers in Washington.

Kendrick is young, twenty-four years of age, a handicap that he partially offsets by wearing a small moustache. He is also a portly young man, a characteristic he offsets by an erect carriage. He has big, impressive plans that materialize at an alarming rate. Under his direction, more than a million dollars soon poured into Knox County to speed the day of the Great Society. And more was on the way. The local staff for this operation moved quickly from the upstairs of a rickety building to occupy the top floor of Barbourville's new, modern City Hall. The downstairs offices are devoted

to the conventional functions of city government, which in a pinch could
be conducted in a telephone booth.

The War on Poverty in Knox County requires skilled mercenaries, trained
people in many fields to cope with the odious ignorance and need that
shroud the hills. An effort to recruit these—or as many as possible—from
local ranks was being made. Advertisements were run in newspapers and
magazines, and the response was encouraging. Many are willing to fight
for pay.

On a summer evening, about forty of these hopefuls gathered in the
second-floor courtroom in the new City Hall—all applicants for jobs in
the war. Among them were teachers who had served time in the remote
one-room schools, and a general cross section of the locally unemployed
and dissatisfied. They sat and listened as Kendrick explained the program.

There will be community centers in the hollows, he said; and youth
activities and early childhood programs, a Head Start program, health programs, general counseling, psychological counseling, a health clinic, family
counseling, demonstrations in skills ranging from sewing to carpentry, and
advice on child rearing, home budgeting, and health. And more.

The assembled job seekers sat impatiently in the red leather chairs, which
smelled new and indicative of the changing times, and waited. At length
they were permitted to ask questons.

"What's the maximum pay?"

"There will be some pay negotiations going on, won't there?"

"Are we going to visit families . . . like casework, like welfare?"

Kendrick said that much of the staff of nearly two hundred which he
envisioned at the time would have to be recruited elsewhere.

As the session continued, the summer sun was gradually ending its day,
and a blue haze was settling over the hills visible outside the big windows
to the east and north. The questions in the courtroom had the ring of conversation about some distant land. But if you looked out the window, you
could see the blue hills that sheltered the hollows along which the creek
called Stinking flows. Brace yourself, Speed Sizemore and Gilbert Bargo
and Ellis Messer. Prepare yourself, Henry Brown and Truman Messer and
Preacher Marsee. The war is nearer than you think.

The programs sprang up quickly as the federal grants were made. Initial
grants indicated by their size that this was no minor war. For the Neighborhood Youth Corps, $144,000; for the Head Start program, $210,000; for
the Unemployed Fathers program, $300,000.

And there is talk of other battles for affluence—a training center to teach operators of heavy equipment, a rural housing proposal that envisions apartments "out by the main roads"; roadway and waterway improvement.

The Barbourville *Mountain Advocate,* the folksy little weekly newspaper that serves Knox County, found poverty fighting a news development rivaling the traditional reporting of basketball games and obituaries. In the column written by the editor, there appeared this observation:

> Young people are humming around the Economic Opportunity offices in city municipal building, because several good jobs are open. You can see a difference in the city building, because most of the second floor will be taken over by these offices.

And almost every issue contained headlines atop the dispatches from the front:

NEW FULL-TIME CHILD WELFARE WORKER
NAMED FOR KNOX COUNTY FOR FIRST TIME

PROJECT HEAD START
GETS APPROVAL

NEIGHBORHOOD YOUTH CORPS PROGRAM
APPROVED AND COUNTY TO GET $162,590

$261,000 MORE FOR NEIGHBORHOOD YOUTH

LARGE GRANT
APPROVED HERE
FOR VISTA WORK

HELP NEEDED BY OPPORTUNITY COUNCIL

150 EMPLOYED
LOCALLY TO STAFF
E. O. COUNCIL

Stinking Creek itself may change because it is a part of Knox County that has been singled out as a battleground in the war. Perhaps it will change completely; perhaps it will revert to its historic patterns—as it did after the other wars and the coal booms. It will take some years before we know.

Irma Gall, the teacher from Lend A Hand, has been recruited for the war, and now has an office in the upstairs array of rooms that house the command post. Some of the people along the creek who are not quite ready to listen to the "outsiders" will listen to Irma. Perhaps she will be instrumental in speeding the surrender of poverty.

The old stone building that housed one-room Messer School, at the junction of Laurel Creek and Stinking Creek, was made into a community center. Many of the young people of Stinking Creek now gather there and are busy refurbishing it. On the Fourth of July, about two hundred people turned out for a picnic and afternoon of singing, a cracker-eating contest and talent show. It got the center off to a momentous beginning, an event that will not soon be forgotten on Stinking Creek.

There is some enthusiasm among the people; there is also some discontent. At a horseshoe-pitching contest at the new community center, a burly young man complained: "Goddammit these horseshoes. I can do this at home. What I hurt for is a job."

But there is some fun at the center, as well as laughter and something to do for the young people. It is not as Virginia Sizemore fears, as she sits on her porch and worries about her Maker. She had said: "I heered they get drunk there. I guess they do." But they don't.

In keeping with the Office of Economic Opportunity's policy of letting the local people have a voice in their victory over want, a council was formed to run the one-room center. Twenty-two-year-old Escoe Smith was elected president, and justified the faith in his leadership and business acumen by quickly organizing a full program for the young people and installing a coin-operated pop machine on the front porch of his home, which is across the road from the center.

The troops of the expeditionary force against poverty are, of course, a big, unwieldy citizen army. And their way is not smooth. Up the hollows where the people watch silently as the platoons of strangers invade their hills, rumors are repeated again and again:

"I hear some of the Vista's been in mental hospitals."

"It's about all beatniks down there, ain't it?"

There was glee when a Vista Volunteer's car was taken away from him after a series of mishaps on the mountain roads; and again when a local boy clubbed a poverty worker on the head with an empty pop bottle.

One mountain family, in whose modest home a Vista Volunteer was billeted, complained that he was sometimes filthy and dressed indecently. A teacher reported that mountain woman were appalled when a Vista Volunteer showed up with "long hair and tight britches. We associate that with prostitution."

A dynamite blast was set off once against a community center, but most people feel that it was some obscure personal objection rather than an expression of general community disapproval.

The unemployed fathers, who work at roads and creek banks and are paid $1.25 an hour, are scornfully called "Happy Pappies" by the few who earn their living without welfare—and by some who gain their living through welfare.

Many of the young boys are finding less leisure time to meditate on the feed sacks at Messer's store since they are now members of the Neighborhood Youth Corps. Part-time jobs are found for them, and in the summer months they can earn $60 a week. During the school term they earn $12.50. Many save the money or spend it wisely. But there always will be a few backsliders, such as the youth who began to ride to school in a taxi and the boy who bought a transistor radio with his first check and a wristwatch with the second.

The reinforced battalions of poverty workers continue to arrive. On one afternoon, in a little restaurant in Barbourville, fourteen newly arrived Vista Volunteers came in. All were to be assigned to hollows in the area. Behind them came an intense youth, fresh from Columbia University graduate school, whose job was to file daily reports on the progress of the Vistas. On the heels of the reporter came another young man, a student of anthropology, whose assigned task was to photograph the Vistas as they were being reported upon. One immediate effect of the War of Poverty is a decided increase in patrons for the local restaurants.

Most of the newcomers give you a valid reason for being there: "I'm terribly interested in these people."

The interests vary. One Vista's avowed goal was to be invited to see "the snake handlers in action."

These shortcomings of the invaders of Stinking Creek are easy to evaluate. What is much more difficult to evaluate fairly are the results of the determined work some of the young people are doing, results that will not be known immediately.

Some mountain people are beginning to put their garbage in closed containers. Parents, patiently wheedled and coaxed, send children back to school. Curiosity and ambition bloom in a child here and there. These are tiny, faltering steps on the uncharted highway to the Great Society. And there are many, many more steps to be taken.

12 Easter Sunday

LONG BEFORE EASTER Sunday, the redbud trees bloomed. The twisted, gnarled black branches, which somehow always manage to affect an appearance of death, sprouted tiny clusters of delicate lavender blooms; the blooms multiplied and deepened into a rich blaze of purple both majestic and delicate. The trees on the mountainside waved under the warming sun and signaled down to the people along the hollow that spring had come.

Most of the small fields, perched haphazardly in the narrow bottoms along the creek, were plowed by now, the stony soil laid bare to receive its commitment of potatoes, squash, beans, and corn.

If hope is ever felt generally along the banks of Stinking Creek, it is at Easter. The sulfurous coal fires in the shallow fireplaces can be put to death; the doors of the cabins can be thrown open; and small, vague hopes can be permitted a brief intrusion upon the spirit.

The congregation of Salem Baptist Church began to arrive early at the small white church on Easter morning. There were more people than usual, more neckties than usual, more smiles than usual. Most had lived through the winter, so it was time to rejoice and give thanks.

Long before Preacher Marsee arrived, barreling up the gravel road in his Oldsmobile F-85, the choir was singing lustily behind the pulpit. The older people were gathering in the pews, and the young boys were flocked around the door. As the choir sang, there was a soft thumping of shoes on the wooden church floor, and occasionally a boy outside would snatch up a few words of the hymn and join the singers for a brief phrase or two.

The hymn was one of hope, and the spectacularly hued redbud trees on the mountain behind the church waved in the wind, as though in time and in accord with the words of the song:

> *"Everybody will be happy . . . will be happy . . . over there,*
> *We will shout and sing His praises over there."*

183

The church door was left open, and the wind that strayed fretfully along the hollow was warm and gentle as it moved in through the door in occasional puffs.

"I will not be a stranger when I get to that city.
There will be friends there to greet me."

The volume increased as the worshipers came into the little church in increasing numbers, until all were in except the boys, who made their traditional late entrance and fell into the rear pew as Preacher Marsee strode to the front. The preacher joined in the final words of the hymn, beaming and nodding:

"I'm acquainted with the folks over there.
I will feel right at home over there,
With the loved ones whose memory I hold,
There will be no lonely days over there . . . over there.
There'll be no stormy weather, but a great get-together . . ."

It was a sermon Preacher Marsee loved to preach: his creed, his entire being, his message, his year-long dream. It was Easter and the time to mark the Resurrection. The time to speak of the force that sustains the religion of Stinking Creek. The ultimate promise. The reason for being.

Preacher Marsee needed no notes. He sprang immediately to the heart of his sermon.

"Surely of all people we are most blessed this morning. We this morning can say something they could not say nineteen hundred and sixty-five years ago." His voice rose along with his extended right hand, and he cried, "When they went to that grave and looked inside. Huh. They said, 'He's not here.' Huh. But this morning we can say, 'He's here!'

"Today He is at the right hand of the Father, making intercessions for us. It is a garntee that we will rise. That some spirit will quicken us. Whooo. You can say that because Christ lives, I shall live also."

The voice fell to a whisper, and Preacher Marsee leaned forward over the wooden pulpit:

"Let's not miss heaven. Ah, let's not miss it, brother. All this world's silver and gold is not worth one minute of heaven."

And then he paused and asked the congregation, "Are there any requests for prayer here this morning?" Half a dozen hands shot up, and there was a chorus of fervent voices asking, "Pray for me." The congregation prayed—together and aloud—a tide of pleading from which an occasional word rose to be distinguished from the rumble of voices: "Father . . . bless

. . . we pray." All punctuated occasionally by the thud of a calloused fist into the seat of a pew.

Preacher Marsee returned quickly to his message. Attacked it directly, strayed to make a point, leaped back to the miracle of life after death, reminisced, and pleaded for all present to follow him into the great promise offered mankind.

"The apostles suffered. They believed. I hope that deep in you you'll accept it this morning.

"We think this morning on the greatest event the world has ever seen, the Ressurection of Jesus Chirst. Huh. Think about that this morning. How much a part of you is this thing we are talking about!"

Preacher Marsee fell silent for a few brief moments. When he spoke again his voice was soft and his eyes were fixed on the open door at the rear of the church, as though talking to some unannounced visitor out there in the sunshine, seen only by him.

"In my mind, this morning, I went up Big Brush Creek. In my mind I went up all the hollows where we have buried our people. In my mind I visited the graves of my five brothers . . . the grave of my wife." He made a gesture with his right hand, as though meticulously picking up tiny objects. And he said, "I picked up the gravels and the weeds from around the graves."

The voice climbed back, strongly and surely. "Your bodies will soon be resting out there. There will be many tears." Someone sobbed hollowly, and Preacher Marsee hesitated briefly, his arm upraised, at the sound of anquish. Then the arm flailed down. "There will be many heartaches."

Both hands gripped the podium, driving the color from the long fingers.

"Death, where is thy sting?

"One day it's all going to be over. I can imagine what's gonna happen that morning . . . on these hillsides . . . where our people are buried.

"Whooo! The dead in Christ are going to be coming out of these hills. I won't be surprised, brother, if they come singing that old song 'Amazing Grace.' The old ship of Zion is going to pass this way. Huh.

"How marvelous it is this morning that we have all these things!

"We can go back in our minds to where Paul preached.

"My Lord and my God! Down all through the ages we see men chopping down cords of wood and stone, and we haven't seen Christ. Huh. We don't have to worry about getting up on that morning. We are already saved in Jesus Christ.

"Isn't it marvelous, as here we go down through the centuries and can testify?

"I see a man thrown into the lion's den, and I know God is coming. Huh."

The words echoed around the little church, then died, and Preacher Marsee pointed a finger steadily around the congregation and promised, "If you're saved you're part of that kingdom."

Preacher Marsee was gazing out the open door again, out into the yellow sunshine.

"I see men who faced cannibals. I see men tied to stakes. Huh. I see men spill their last drop of blood . . . and they knew the Lord was coming.

"A million years from now, when this world is over, we will go out there . . . .

"If He can make a mind strong enough to break a sound barrier, to enjoy music . . . whoo . . . I can see my Lord over there this morning. Sittin' there. Isn't that marvelous, brother?" With the question, he turned to Gobel Mills, tall, erect, clad in spotless pressed khaki shirt and trousers, sitting on the preacher's left. Gobel Mills, long a leader at Salem Baptist Church, nodded in agreement. But it was not his voice that answered, "Marvelous, brother."

Preacher Marsee threw his head back, the veins straining in his neck, the head rolling slowly from side to side as though driven by some personal ecstasy.

"I thank Him for the food I eat, for the clothes I wear."

The head came down; the clear eyes were fixed on the congregation.

"He came forth in that power. He broke the Roman seal. He rolled away that stone. I can take you to a flat place in the mountains, almost as flat as this floor, where a man can walk as far as Ellis' house over there.

"One-ton rocks were there. Some weighed five tons . . . ten tons. Huh.

"I see men fall on their knees. I see them cry out. I know the Ressurrection took place. They know Christ was crucifiied. They know God tore those rocks apart.

"Oh, be born again. It's a greater miracle than those trees blooming out there. It's a garntee that every man, woman, and child will be tried. He will judge the world in righteousness. He'll judge you for every sin of your life. Huh. He'll judge that very soul of yours.

"God gave assurance to all men when He raised Jesus from the dead."

Preacher Marsee paused, looked toward the floor, and shook his head from side to side, a gesture of wonder.

"Some men were locked in a submarine, and they tapped out a message: 'Is there any hope?' Nobody asks, 'Is there any hope?' this morning.

"Think about being locked forever in the darkness of a never-ending eternity.

"On this Easter, only Christ can save you. Huh. Oh, God of Abraham, Jacob, and Moses! Let Him do this for you this morning.

"What would you do if you knew this was your last meeting? If you knew you were going to stand before the Judge?

"I see men hurt and lying on the highways, crying and begging for one more chance to get back to the church."

Preacher Marsee waved a thin arm slowly in a wide arc that took in every member of the congregation. "Do what you believe you'd do if this was the last time you and I attended Salem Church. Do what you think the Lord would want you to do."

After Gilbert Bargo had carefully stacked and put away the $15.50 collection, the preacher prayed:

"I put all I got in this Lord. These things are coming. We are living in that day when people grow cold and indifferent . . . in that day when people up and down this hollow are concerned with things that give pleasure.

"We live in a day when grocers weigh out groceries and nobody tells the customers the weight on God's scales.

"Oh, Father, we don't believe we've got much time left. Whatever strength you give us, whatever days you give us, they are going to be for you.

"May we hear you say, 'You tried'?

"If you count us worthy, bless us. Go with us now. Give us another chance. Amen."

And the tiny church was filled with the earnest, answering voices: "Amen."

13 Epilogue—Sometimes in the Night

WHAT IS THE hillbilly's future?

There is no simple answer because each man, woman, and child living in the hidden hollows of Appalachia is a unique human being, a fact that has escaped some who study and ponder and count and categorize the hillbilly. He lives in a land that seems never to change, yet undergoes subtle daily changes.

Mary Sizemore sued for divorce from the man who occasionally came down the road in the black Pontiac. She also "got on the welfare for $118 a month."

Stoney, Henry Brown's youngest, enrolled in the Head Start program at the new brick elementary school in DeWitt.

Ellis Messer, carefully recording the volume of his business in his blue notebook, must go to court. Elected to the fiscal court in the fall general elections, he was one of the winners challenged in a rash of suits charging illegal voting. Hobert Mills lost the race for jailer, so Peggy did not move to Barbourville where the courteous town boys would open doors for her.

Alex School was closed by the county board of education. And so was Messer. But Shady School continued to thwart the beautiful children of Stinking Creek.

Of all the questions to be asked of the hillbilly's future, the most vital and far-reaching must be asked of the War on Poverty. Will it succeed? It will make poverty more comfortable, but more than that, it offers the first exciting hope of accomplishing a greater good. Kentucky, already third behind only California and New York in the cost of poverty programs, expected to obtain around $100,000,000 annually in federal money to fight poverty. Knox County, with its 25,000 people, planned to spend $2,000,000 of this each year.

188

In Appalachia, in a thousand hollows, the War on Poverty comes directly into contact with the hillbilly through the hordes of eager, sincere, and dedicated young people of the Vista Volunteers, the Appalachian Volunteers, and similar groups. Many college students devote weekend after weekend to working with children and adults in the remote areas. Already, some accomplishments are heartening.

As a result of these lonely but magnificent battles, often fought by young people who come to Appalachia completely unfamiliar with the ways of the mountains, the first significant change in the hillbilly's mind has miraculously occurred.

That change is to the beginning of a belief.

The hillbilly believes. He believes the promises. For generations he has not believed. His history has been one of futility, trickery, lies.

He learned to distrust the plantation masters to the east. He learned that the Indian, the beasts, and the forest were enemies. He learned that coal was not a blessing, but a curse to entomb him beneath the earth, to shatter his bones and maim his body. He learned that the absentee owners of his natural wealth would lie, use him, and desert him. He learned that the unions he bled for would turn away in his hour of need. He learned that his political leaders would never honor their promises of roads, jobs, and decent schools. He learned that the railroads brought, not prosperity for him, but only plunderers.

History must judge the still-new War on Poverty, its cost, its effectiveness, its blunders, its achievements. But whatever is decided in the years to come, it must be written that for the first time in generations, the hillbilly has believed.

The young volunteer workers arrive bubbling with enthusiasm and un-encumbered with any notions of how civic, political, or social agencies function traditionally. They go directly to the hollows, usually moving into a tiny cabin with a local family.

Soon, long-idle men are cleaning a cemetery or repairing a road. Adults, their meager education long tossed into disuse, huddle late at night, listening intently to college-age strangers who teach them spelling, simple mathematics and even Kentucky history.

In one hollow, a young Jewish girl from Connecticut sits on a sagging porch helping break green beans for the dinner pot. Before she leaves, a plan for community garbage disposal is born.

In another hollow, a slender college student from Oregon heaves huge stones from a neglected roadway. One by one, these who use the road join him, until a crew of twenty men are laboring and smiling in the dust and heat. Before the road project is completed, there is agreement upon a community effort to clean up an abandoned school and rebuild it into a recreational center.

Are these more false prophets sent to disillusion? More and more hillbillies are convinced that they are not.

The Community Action Programs, of course, are born and thrive on red tape and mounds of senseless paper work. But they too, in hollow after hollow, are finding believers. Health and sanitation are being discussed; there is talk of agriculturally related businesses—tractor repair shops, feed stores—new ways to find economic salvation. The hillbilly is shown how to make use of the web of federal and state agencies that already existed but which he never understood.

And for the first time, startled legislators are finding that their mail brings demands from remote communities never considered important enough to be included on the campaign trail. The poor are learning to speak with the voice promised them by the Office of Economic Opportunity.

This new voice does not bring universal rejoicing. Those of the established power structures sometimes find the voice ominous. A county official drummed short, fat fingers on his worn oak desk and predicted, "My God, we're all going to be run by a welfare-supported power structure."

There is even hope for the abused land. Kentucky, with the driving evangelism of the converted backslider, finally stirred itself legislatively. Tougher, more practical laws to control strip mining of coal were rushed onto the books by legislators smarting under the lashing of newspapers, vocal conservationists, and threats of more stringent action from Washington. There is a hope that the waste and overburden from the mines now will not find their way to the streams to pollute, silt, and kill all vegetable and marine life.

More and more coal is being mined by the large "captive mines" operated by major national companies. These are efficient, safe, and modern. Men earn good salaries there, and the control of waste materials is admirable.

The biggest promise to the curtailing of destruction of the hills lies in the atom. More and more, large electrical power-generating plants are finding the atom the more economical fuel. And the demand for coal for the huge steam generators may someday dwindle to nothing.

But someday Americans will discover what has happened to the hills. And on that day, who will explain away the monstrous ruin of the land and streams?

Here and there are those who point the way to healing the sickened land and rivers. The United States Forest Service has reclaimed small streams that now flow cleanly between stabilized banks free of silt and sulfur. To these healed streams, the fish have returned.

Reforestation of the denuded hills is under way in many areas. The "happy pappies" who shuffle along the hellish strip-mine cuts and poke pine seedlings into the ground may be creating green, lush vistas for their grandchildren to behold. Above all, East Kentucky has scenic beauty and as yet unharnessed rivers. There is talk of lakes and dams for generating power. Recreational use of the hills is increasing.

All these plans and projects and hopes and promises raise complex and vital questions about the hillbilly's future.

The smaller questions persist, too.

Will Fred Brown get on the "project work"?

Will Rosie Brown and Floyd Brown reconcile their differences so Floyd can leave his ridiculous little shack up Johns Branch and return to his woman?

Will Henry Brown succeed in getting Fred's powerful horse?

And who will answer to the boys lounging on the feed sacks at Messer's store? And who will cherish Peggy Mills and Judy Warren?

What forgiveness is there for sinful Gilbert Bargo who clutches his small calloused hands in supplication in Salem Baptist Church and secretely lusts for an inch of rich topsoil for his steep farm?

Who will weep for Virginia Sizemore if she sits alone and never hears the call to handle serpents?

Indeed, what is a hillbilly?

He is, in some ways, all these people. Perhaps he should not be completely changed. Perhaps he clings to characteristics that may hold some value for us all. Should we stamp out his love of family? And what of the young men? On Stinking Creek there are no muggings, robberies, stabbings, rapes. Yet every boy carries a pocket knife—not as a weapon, but as a symbol of responsible manhood. On Stinking Creek you can leave your car unlocked with its load of cameras, typewriter, and personal belongings without fear. Where else can you do this?

On Stinking Creek there is a religion, a literal, firm belief in a God who will someday command the huge, hard sandstone boulders to split apart and summon the dead to rejoice in the everlasting Resurrection. Is there anything to be learned here?

During the year of the gathering of this book people asked:

"Are you talking with the educational leaders?"

"Are you talking with the political leaders?"

"Are you talking with the officials in the War on Poverty?"

And the answer was No.

One talks with Henry Brown and Gilbert Bargo and Preacher Marsee and Hobert Mills and Floyd Brown. One talks with the children as they squirm in Shady School or reach into the red cooler full of pop in Messer's store.

The educational philosophy of Knox County, Kentucky, is to be seen in Shady School. You see the attitude of the political leaders as you walk up the creek—many times to the marshy beginning of it.

Where are the answers?

Perhaps each hillbilly must find his own. Perhaps the answers lie in the increased affluence of the poverty-stricken as the crisp checks from Washington and Frankfort increase in size. Perhaps answers lie in Preacher Marsee's fifteen-dollar sermons in Salem Baptist Church. Perhaps part of the answer lies in a crumpled note written by a little girl named Linda Sue one day in Shady School. Down at the bottom of the page she wrote a four-letter word:

"Love."

Perhaps an old mountaineer far up Middle Fork solved part of the problem when he was questioned. As he sought for an answer he scratched himself somewhere deep in the folds of his faded Washington Dee Cee overalls, stared frankly, and then said:

"Peers to me like it's a matter of whether you'd druther have a bathroom or a whole mountain to pee on."

Sometimes in the night the questions come back to haunt the mind.

A taxpayer may hope the millions are spent wisely in Knox County. A Christian may hope Preacher Marsee is right. But anyone must hope that the people who live along Stinking Creek find what they are seeking—and have been seeking ever since their ancestors left the debtor prisons and filthy streets of England. And the most fervent hope of all is that they need not journey to Detroit or Cleveland or Chicago to find it, but find it on Stinking Creek.